JDBC: Practical Guide for Java Programmers

The Morgan Kaufmann Practical Guides Series
Series Editor: Michael J. Donahoo

JDBC: Practical Guide for Java Programmers
Gregory D. Speegle

TCP/IP Sockets in Java: Practical Guide for Programmers
Kenneth L. Calvert and Michael J. Donahoo

TCP/IP Sockets in C: Practical Guide for Programmers
Michael J. Donahoo and Kenneth L. Calvert

For further information on these books and for a list of forthcoming titles,
please visit our Web site at *www.mkp.com*.

JDBC: Practical Guide for Java Programmers

Gregory D. Speegle

Baylor University

MORGAN KAUFMANN PUBLISHERS

AN IMPRINT OF ACADEMIC PRESS

A Harcourt Science and Technology Company

SAN FRANCISCO   SAN DIEGO   NEW YORK   BOSTON
LONDON   SYDNEY   TOKYO

Senior Editor Rick Adams
Publishing Services Manager Scott Norton
Assistant Publishing Services Manager Edward Wade
Assistant Acquisitions Editor Karyn Johnson
Project Management Sarah Burgundy
Cover Design Matt Seng, Seng Design
Cover Image Photodisc
Text Design Side by Side Studios / Mark Ong
Composition/Illustration Windfall Software, using ZzTEX
Copyeditor Sharilyn Hovind
Proofreader Melissa Maristuen
Indexer Steve Rath
Printer Edwards Brothers

Designations used by companies to distinguish their products are often claimed as trademarks or registered trademarks. In all instances in which Morgan Kaufmann Publishers is aware of a claim, the product names appear in initial capital or all capital letters. Readers, however, should contact the appropriate companies for more complete information regarding trademarks and registration.

Morgan Kaufmann Publishers
340 Pine Street, Sixth Floor, San Francisco, CA 94104-3205, USA
http://www.mkp.com

ACADEMIC PRESS
A Harcourt Science and Technology Company
525 B Street, Suite 1900, San Diego, CA 92101-4495, USA
http://www.academicpress.com

Academic Press
Harcourt Place, 32 Jamestown Road, London, NW1 7BY, United Kingdom
http://www.academicpress.com

06 05 04 03 02   5 4 3 2 1

Library of Congress Control Number: 2001094350
ISBN: 1-55860-736-6

Transferred to Digital Printing 2007

Contents

Preface

Software development is as much art as science. Thus, in order to master a particular technology, it is not sufficient to merely study it in texts; it is mandatory to use the technology in a project. Unfortunately, in the current educational system, it is difficult to provide both the theoretical concepts required for learning and the technical details required to complete a project. Likewise, in today's fast-moving information technology industry, it is difficult for practitioners to evaluate new developments because of the steep learning curve required to understand each new area.

One example of a difficult technology to master is JDBC, the application programming interface (API) for connecting Java programs with database systems. The API is quote large—a printout of the online documentation would be over 100 pages long—and nearly impossible to cover in an academic course or for programmers to learn in their spare time. However, in order to use Java programs to access the vast amounts of information in database systems, students and other programmers have to learn these details. Thus, this guide focuses on the important concepts of JDBC, allowing users to digest key components without having to initially wade through myriad details.

The purpose of this guide is to provide students and practitioners with enough information to create projects using JDBC. It is designed to get the reader up and running as soon as possible. The possible uses for this book are many: It can be used as a supplemental text for an upper-level or graduate database course or Java course. It can serve as a quick means to evaluate JDBC as a possible alternative for an information technology company. Finally, it can serve as an introduction to JDBC for programmers looking to learn new skills.

Since the guide is designed for quick exposure to JDBC, it assumes several capabilities of the reader: 1) knowledge of SQL, at least at the level of simple SQL commands; 2) an understanding of the basics of database design, such as schema, table, and foreign key constraints; 3) enough familiarity with the operating system to install any needed software or find needed files; and 4) a basic understanding of Java. All of the Java related to JDBC is explained and concepts like applets, frames, graphic user interface (GUI), classes, and so on are presented as needed for completeness, but they are not explained in detail. If you need additional information on Java, there are several good texts, such as [2].

Using this Guide

A common lament among computer professionals unfamiliar with Java and databases is that setting up the environment is not straightforward. For both databases and Java, this is the price for working on many different platforms. The guide Web site (*cs.baylor.edu/~speegle/pockjdbc*) provides two different means for loading information into databases and some basic information on making a system work with JDBC. However, not all systems are covered. It is important to have access to individuals or reference materials for needed configuration information. Specifically, you will need to know the name of the jar file containing a special JDBC class called the *Driver*. You will also have to know the specific name of the *Driver* for your database. All JDBC drivers require a structured name to find the database, and you will need to know this for your database as well. The example ConnectionJDBC (see Section 1.2) uses this information and can be easily modified to work in a different environment. Once ConnectionJDBC is modified, the rest of the examples should work with your driver/database combination, unless the example uses a feature not supported by your setup.

Programming Conventions

This guide uses several conventions for describing programming constructs. First, all methods are followed by () to distinguish them from constants and variables. Second, all methods that are part of the Java 2 Standard Edition, Version 1.3, are in italics, while methods in the program examples are in plain text. Whenever a method in the Software Development Kit (SDK) is overridden, italics are used to refer to the original method, while plain text is used to refer to the specific methods in the program examples. Classes all begin with capital letters, with Java classes again in italics. Constants are in all capital letters, and Java constants are in italics. Database tables and fields are in plain type. The programs contain minimal comments, but each line is numbered. Discussion in the text refers to the line numbers for easy reference. This is intentional, as some of the constructs used in the examples need significant explanation and should not be used without careful consideration of the issues.

Chapter Overview

All of the examples in this guide are motivated by a video rental business called eVid. The book consists of seven chapters and an appendix. Chapter 1 introduces JDBC and the database used by the program examples. It also contains an analogy that compares JDBC programming to running a store. The examples in Chapter 1 introduce basic JDBC constructs needed by anyone wanting to connect a database to a Java program. Chapter 2 presents four different ways to display responses to a query from a database. Three of these examples use a GUI, while the fourth stores the results as a file. Chapter 3 covers the different ways the same query can be asked. Included in this chapter is an example of using stored procedures with JDBC. Chapter 4

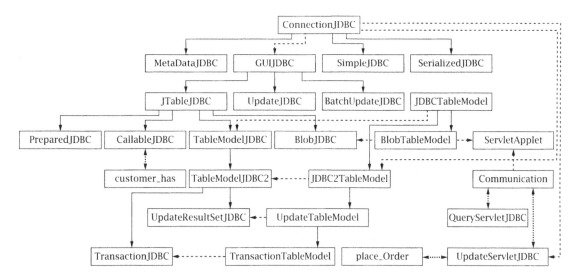

Figure 1: Class Hierarchy Diagram

contains three programs examples showing how to update the database. There are two special update modes covered, including batch updates, in which many updates can be grouped into one database update. Chapter 5 covers four advanced topics that might not apply to everyone, but will prove crucial if an application requires the information. This chapter covers drivers in detail, metadata, transactions, and binary large objects (as an example of an SQL3 data type). Chapter 6 brings the entire book into focus by showing an application example. The application contains an applet front-end and two servlet back-end classes, along with stored procedures for a true three-tiered application. Chapter 7 briefly touches on the parts of JDBC not covered in the rest of the guide, as well as some important additional issues. The appendix contains code used by some of the other examples, but since the code is not directly JDBC related, it is not discussed.

After you read Chapter 1, you can read the remaining chapters in almost any order. The program examples do build on other pieces, but each chapter emphasizes new concepts while only briefly referencing information found elsewhere. As such, you can extract the information you need in a nonlinear fashion. The classes defined in the examples are strongly interrelated. Figure 1 shows how these relationships work.

Web Resource

There is a large amount of related information on the book's Web site, *cs.baylor.edu/~speegle /pockjdbc*. All of the program examples can be downloaded, as well as the database example. In addition, there are links to JDBC-related information, such as the Sun online JDBC API documentation. Any errata and contributions by others will also be listed there.

Programming is an art, so it is likely that there are bugs in the examples presented in this guide. It could be that the bugs only appear in certain environments or under certain conditions, but naturally I do not expect the code to be perfect. However, with your help, I'm hoping it can become better. I look forward to finding out what works and what doesn't under the many different environments possible for JDBC. If you have any comments or suggestions for improvement, please contact me through my email address, available on the Web site. Also, on the site is a link to Reader Contributions, where such improvements will be posted.

JDBC versus Other Options

The primary use for the examples in this guide will be allowing users to interact with a database over the Internet. There are several competing mechanisms to allow programmers to do this, so a natural question is Why JDBC? (And related to that, Why this guide?) In order to answer these questions, I will present some alternatives and point out several reasons for choosing JDBC.

Common Gateway Interface.   The common gateway interface (CGI) is the oldest method for connecting the Internet to a database. Under CGI, a program, often written in a scripting language such as Perl—but C and C++ are also possible—is executed by the Web server whenever a request for a particular page is received. The Web server would pass to the program all of the available information either as environment variables, or as standard input. The program would generate the response, usually in Hypertext Markup Language (HTML), and the data would be sent to the requesting site.

Databases can connect to the Internet with this framework by using embedded Structure Query Language (SQL) in the C++ program or libraries for the scripting languages. Such a program would be very similar to a typical embedded-SQL application, except that the results would be HTML instead of either graphic data or a report.

The advantage of this approach is that the technology is widely supported. Almost all Web servers support CGI and almost all databases support embedded SQL in C or C++ programs. The disadvantage of CGI systems is that the systems are not at all portable. The programs would have to be modified if they are moved to another machine or if another database is used. The CGI system is also not able to take advantage of any Web server features. Finally, each call to a CGI program is a distinct process. This greatly increases the number of processes running on a server.

Active Server Pages.   Another popular solution is based on using a combination of products available from Microsoft. It is called active server pages (ASP). ASP allows the creation of dynamic Web page content. ASP uses a scripting language, either VBScript or JavaScript to create the Web page. In order for ASP to access a database, open database connectivity (ODBC) and activeX data objects (ADO) are required. ASP can also use component object model (COM) to create objects to improve the performance of the code and to provide additional functionality.

Under ASP, a call is made to a Web server requesting a page with dynamic content. The script in ASP is invoked, and any database calls are passed through to the database via ADO and ODBC. The biggest advantage of ASP is that it is supported by many Internet service providers [1]. JDBC has two advantages over ASP-based systems. First, ASP has limited support in operating systems other than Microsoft Windows. Second, the different components require learning distinct paradigms in order to work with them successfully. ASP itself is scriptlike, while ODBC is more like C++ and COM is yet a different object paradigm [6].

PHP. Another option is PHP, described on the Web site *php.com* as a "server-side cross-platform, HTML embedded scripting language." PHP allows dynamic Web content by using scripting commands similar to ASP and JSP. You can also connect to a database using PHP commands and perform SQL queries. PHP is supported by many Web servers and databases, thus providing it with the benefits of the other approaches. JDBC has an advantage over PHP in that complex objects can be passed to applets within the Java framework, while PHP is restricted to HTML. (Further information is available on PHP at *php.com*.)

Acknowledgments

This work would not have been possible without the support of a large number of people. First and foremost, I want to thank my wife, Laura, and my children, Mark and Erica, who were very patient putting up with a grumpy husband and father during the writing of this book. Next, I want to thank the technical editor of the Pocket Series, Dr. Jeff Donahoo, for encouraging me to write it in the first place. I would also like to thank the Department of Computer Science faculty (*cs.baylor.edu*) and the School of Engineering and Computer Science at Baylor University. Much of this work was accomplished during my sabbatical, and I could not have completed it without that time to write. Thanks also goes to the people at Morgan Kaufmann for publishing the book, especially Karyn Johnson, who had to put up with a lot of ignorant questions. And I want to thank the Texas-Life Insurance Company, which has provided projects and resources for students in my senior database class, including recent ones on JDBC. They also provided resources that helped in the writing of this book. Finally, I want to thank the reviewers, Guillermo Francia, Vijay Kumar, Paul Fortier, Salih Yurttas, Robert Brunner, Bill Grosky, and Bharat Sharma, as well as the students already using this text, who have provided invaluable insights into the program examples it offers.

chapter 1

Introduction to JDBC

JDBC is an API defined in the java.sql and javax.sql packages for connecting an arbitrary database to a Java program. Although it is a common misconception, JDBC is not an acronym for anything. Like the Java Development Kit (JDK), the JDBC API has been revised over time. The proposed final draft of JDBC 3.0 was released on October 26, 2000, but this guide uses the more widely supported JDBC 2.1 API. In the proposal for JDBC 3.0, there are 19 interfaces, 6 classes, and 4 exception classes.

The very high ratio of interfaces to classes (3:1, as opposed to java.awt with a ratio of 1:5) allows the JDBC API to have tremendous flexibility. Effectively, every vendor is allowed to implement the interfaces to best communicate with a particular database or set of databases. This is explained in much more detail in Section 5.1, but for now, the important point is that communication with a database can be handled by the JDBC API.

1.1   An Analogy

One of the best ways to understand the basic workings of JDBC is to consider an analogy. Let's suppose we operate a small business that sells gadgets. The gadgets are produced in a factory, across a river from our store. Without a boat or a bridge, there is no way for us to get to the factory or for the factory to deliver goods to the store.

This represents the situation with a database and a Java program: the Java program is the store, and the database is the factory. Without something to help, there is no way for the Java program to make requests of the database, and the database cannot communicate with the Java program. In order for products to get from the factory to the store, it would be logical to build a bridge over the river. The analogous piece of software for the Java program and database is an interface called the *driver*. We load a specific driver into a Java program by using the static method *forName()* in the *Class* class. For example, to load the default driver provided with Java 2 Standard Edition, Version 1.3, we would use this method:

```
Class.forName("sun.jdbc.odbc.JdbcOdbcDriver");
```

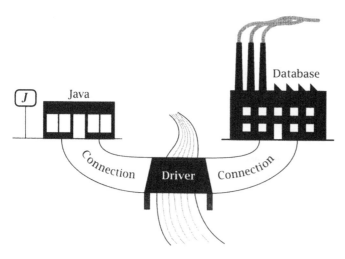

Figure 1.1: Analogy with driver and connection.

Interestingly, this particular driver is called the "bridge," since it spans from JDBC to ODBC (open database connectivity, another generic way to connect to a database [7]). If the driver can't be loaded, a *ClassNotFoundException* is thrown. Fortunately, with the standard driver, this shouldn't happen. Additionally, the driver can be loaded by setting the "jdbc.drivers" property of the Java virtual machine (JVM). The command line option to do this is

```
java -Djdbc.drivers=sun.jdbc.odbc.JdbcOdbcDriver SimpleJDBC
```

where SimpleJDBC is the name of the executing class.

As modern rivers are crossed by many bridges, there are many drivers to connect Java programs to databases. In fact, one Java program can connect to many databases at the same time. This requires a special class to manage the various drivers so that the correct one is used. This class is called the *DriverManager*, and it is a class, not an interface. The *DriverManager* class is implemented as part of Java 2 Standard Edition, Version 1.3, so it is database independent. Furthermore, the *DriverManager* is not instantiated, but rather the static methods of the class are used. Whenever a driver method is needed, the *DriverManager* class selects the appropriate driver from all of the ones loaded. If no driver is appropriate, an *SQLException* is thrown, usually "No suitable driver."

Continuing with the analogy, now that a bridge spans the river, it would be possible to cross from the store to the factory and vice versa. However, without a road, transporting goods would be difficult at best. We need a road between the store and the factory to facilitate transportation. The "road" in JDBC is another interface, called *Connection* (see Figure 1.1).

Just as the road must go across the bridge, the *Connection* interface must be implemented by an object generated by the driver. Now the role of the *DriverManager* comes into play, as the *DriverManager* automatically selects the correct driver for the desired connection. We use the *getConnection( )* method of the *DriverManager* class to find the right connection. The *getConnection( )* method requires a URL telling the *DriverManager* which database and driver to use. The *getConnection( )* method optionally provides a username and password for the database. For example,

```
DriverManager.getConnection("jdbc:odbc:jdbc_book", "jdbc_user", "guest");
```

tells the *DriverManager* we want a driver that can bridge from JDBC to ODBC and that can access the database "jdbc_book" as user "jdbc_user" with password "guest." If we have only loaded the basic driver provided with the Java 2 Standard Edition, Version 1.3, the *DriverManager* will attempt to use that driver for the user "jdbc_user" with password "guest."

There are many possible problems that can arise from the use of the *getConnection( )* method. These problems all throw various *SQLExceptions*. Unfortunately, it is common to get fairly unhelpful exception messages with these types of problems. For example, using the standard driver with MS Access under Windows 2000 produces the message "IO Error" when the user name is incorrect. It's a good idea to run the program with intentional errors in order to learn what error messages a particular driver/database will generate.

Once the bridge and the road are both complete, we can now safely drive to the factory and place our order. The JDBC equivalent to driving to the factory is the *Statement* interface, and an SQL query is our order. We create a *Statement* from our *Connection* object. For example, if dbConnect is the name of our *Connection* object, then

```
dbConnect.createStatement();
```

returns a *Statement* object.

1.2 Connection/Statement Example

The code example for making connections to a database is the class ConnectionJDBC. It contains several similar methods for doing the same thing. This allows us to use the class with different database/driver combinations. The primary method in the class is called makeConnection( ). The method always returns a *Connection* object that is the result of the *DriverManager* method *getConnection*. In order for this example to work, a database must be installed and the appropriate driver files must be available to the JVM. Section 1.3 provides information on the database we use in this guide. Consult the system documentation for other driver/database combinations.

ConnectionJDBC

```
1   import java.sql.*;
2
3   public class ConnectionJDBC {
4
5       public Connection makeConnection()
6           throws SQLException {
```

```
7          try {
8              Class.forName("sun.jdbc.odbc.JdbcOdbcDriver");
9          } catch (ClassNotFoundException e) {
10             throw new SQLException("Unable to load driver class");
11         }
12         return DriverManager.getConnection("jdbc:odbc:jdbc_book");
13     }
14
15     public Connection makeConnection(String URL)
16         throws SQLException {
17         return DriverManager.getConnection(URL);
18     }
19
20     public Connection makeConnection(String DriverName, String URL)
21         throws SQLException {
22         try {
23             Class.forName(DriverName);
24         } catch (ClassNotFoundException e) {
25             throw new SQLException("Unable to load driver class");
26         }
27         return DriverManager.getConnection(URL);
28     }
29
30     public Connection makeConnection(String URL, String username,
31                                     String password)
32         throws SQLException {
33         return DriverManager.getConnection(URL,username,password);
34     }
35
36     public Connection makeConnection(String DriverName, String URL,
37                                     String username, String password)
38         throws SQLException {
39         try {
40             Class.forName(DriverName);
41         } catch (ClassNotFoundException e) {
42             throw new SQLException("Unable to load driver class");
43         }
44         return DriverManager.getConnection(URL,username,password);
45     }
46
47     public void closeConnection(Connection c, Statement s)
48     {
49         try {
50             if (s != null) s.close();
51             if (c != null) c.close();
52         } catch (SQLException sqlex) {}
53     }
```

```
54
55      public static void main(String args[]) {
56          ConnectionJDBC CJ = new ConnectionJDBC();
57          Connection dbConnect = null;
58          Statement dbStatement = null;
59          try {
60              switch (args.length) {
61              case 0 : dbConnect = CJ.makeConnection();
62                  break;
63              case 1 : dbConnect = CJ.makeConnection(args[0]);
64                  break;
65              case 2 : dbConnect = CJ.makeConnection(args[0],args[1]);
66                  break;
67              case 3 : dbConnect = CJ.makeConnection(args[0],args[1],args[2]);
68                  break;
69              case 4 : dbConnect = CJ.makeConnection(args[0],args[1],args[2],
70                                                     args[3]);
71                  break;
72              default :
73                  System.out.println("Using the default driver");
74                  dbConnect = CJ.makeConnection();
75              }
76              System.out.println("Made a connection!");
77              dbStatement = dbConnect.createStatement();
78              System.out.println("Made a statement!");
79          } catch (SQLException sqlex) {
80              System.out.println(sqlex.getMessage());
81          }
82          finally {
83              CJ.closeConnection(dbConnect,dbStatement);
84              System.out.println("Closed the connection.");
85          }
86      }
87  }
```

ConnectionJDBC

The five versions of makeConnection( ) are in lines 5–45. Each of the five methods calls the *getConnection( )* method. In the first three cases (lines 12, 17, and 27), the method receives a parameter describing the database. For the default database, this string is jdbc:odbc:jdbc_ book (line 12). In all other cases, the string is passed in as a parameter. The documentation with a JDBC driver should contain the specifications for this string, and additional information can be found in Section 5.1.

In the other two calls to the *getConnection( )* method (lines 33 and 44), in addition to the database URL, the method accepts a username and password to be sent to the database.

The response to an invalid username and password will vary according to the database/driver combination.

Three of the five methods load a specific driver class into the JVM (lines 8, 23, and 40). This class must be accessible to the JVM, or a *ClassNotFoundException* is thrown. The methods always convert this exception into an *SQLException* (lines 9-11, 24-26, and 41-43). There are two reasons to do this: First, JDBC methods always throw *SQLExceptions*, and this converts the exception into a consistent type. Second, in this case the problem is specifically an inability to find the driver needed for JDBC. The new *SQLException* explicitly states the problem as such, so classes referencing ConnectionJDBC will receive a more accurate exception message.

The other two versions of the method do not load a driver class into the JVM. These methods will only work if either the class is already loaded by a previous call to one of the other methods, or the class is loaded by setting the "jdbc.drivers" property. Otherwise, an *SQLException* with the message "No suitable driver" is thrown.

Lines 47-53 close the connection to the database. Whenever a Java program makes a connection to a database, the database reserves resources for the anticipated requests that are about to arrive. Once a program exits, no further requests will be sent to the database, but the resources may be held for a long time. By closing the connection, these resources are released. In order to close the connection, we first close the *Statement* (line 50). This also closes any *ResultSet* that might be open (see Section 1.4). Once the *Statement* is closed, we close the *Connection* in line 51.

The closeConnection( ) method catches any *SQLExceptions* that may be thrown and effectively disposes of them. We do this for two reasons. First, it simplifies classes using ConnectionJDBC in that database connections can be closed without having to catch exceptions. Second, if there is an exception when closing the connection, there is nothing the JDBC program can do about it, as such exceptions are virtually always the result of communication errors. Clearly, the method should be modified to throw *SQLExceptions* if it is important to know that the connection is closed.

The main( ) method in lines 55-87 primarily tests the possible different types of connections. First, a new ConnectionJDBC object is created (line 56), and then a *Connection* and a *Statement* object are declared. Next, within a *try block*, a switch statement (lines 60-75) uses the number of command line parameters to call a version of the makeConnection( ) method. Line 77 creates the *Statement* object from the *Connection* using the *createStatement( )* method. If there is a problem, the exception is caught in lines 79-81. Line 80 outputs the message associated with the *SQLException*. Another useful method is *printStackTrace( )*, which displays the current line number of all methods on the stack when the exception is thrown. (Note that classes written by users always show line numbers, but for classes in the Java API, line numbers are not always provided.)

Whether or not an exception is thrown, we always want to close the connection to the database. We use the *finally block* to make sure this happens. Lines 82-85 are a typical execution. If the closeConnection( ) method is modified to throw an SQLException, then it must be caught in a nested *try/catch block*. Avoiding this unneeded structure is one of the reasons for catching the exception in the closeConnection( ) method.

Customers		
CustomerID	Int	Primary Key
CustomerName	VarChar	
CustomerAddress	VarChar	
CustomerPhone	VarChar	

Titles		
TitleID	Int	Primary Key
Title	VarChar	
Year	Int	
Price	Float	
URL	VarChar	
Image	BLOB	

Tapes		
TapeID	Int	Primary Key
TitleID	Int	Foreign Key Titles
Type	VarChar	

Orders		
OrderNumber	Int	Primary Key
CustomerID	Int	Foreign Key Customers
TapeID	Int	Foreign Key Tapes
DueDate	Date	
Status	Char	

Figure 1.2: Table schemas.

1.3 Database Example

The basic premise of this guide is that programmers learn by doing. In order to learn JDBC, therefore, we need a database. Our examples are pulled from an imaginary online video rental business called eVid. The eVid database is very simple. It consists of four relations: Customers, Titles, Tapes, and Orders. The schema is outlined in Figure 1.2.

Customers Table.   The Customers table contains all of the information about customers, including names, addresses, and phone numbers. The primary key of the relation is the *CustomerID* field, which would be a unique number like a driver's license number in a real example.

Titles Table.   The Titles table contains information about the different movie titles, such as cost and year made. It also contains a primary key called *TitleID*. The Titles table also contains two special fields. One is called *URL*, a string indicating where an image related to the movie can be downloaded. The *URL* field is a relative location, so it can be used under a variety of conditions. The other field is called *Image* and is BLOB data actually stored in the database. Obviously, this represents some redundancy, as we don't need both the data and a link to the data. However, there are circumstances where the BLOB type can't be used. Thus, by having both fields, we can still do interesting work. Clearly, if a database doesn't support BLOB data, we would use only the *URL* field.

Tapes Table.   The Tapes table contains information about individual physical tapes. A tape has a single title, but eVid will have many tapes for each title. In this case, a "tape" is also either DVD or VHS format. The Tapes table also contains a primary key called *TapeID*. In a real environment, this would be a bar code value affixed to the tape box, or some other physical identifier. The *TitleID* from the Titles table is also part of this table.

Orders Table.   The Orders table connects a customer to a tape and has a date the tape should be returned. The Orders table also contains a primary key called *OrderNumber*. The last field of the order relation is *Status*. Status can have two values, "I" or "O." If a tape is checked out, the status for the order is set to "O." When it is brought back, the status is set to "I." It is easy to see how the status could contain far more values, denoting concepts such as lost, stolen, destroyed, or sold (assuming the video store sells videos).

Although a database is needed, nobody will learn JDBC while they are building tables and loading data. Therefore, the companion Web site contains two important ways to build the database for you. The first is a Microsoft Access database already set up with example tables. It is available at *cs.baylor.edu/~speegle/pockjdbc/jdbc_book.mdb.* For using a different database, there is a set of four files with SQL commands for creating and populating the four tables. They are available at

> *cs.baylor.edu/~speegle/pockjdbc/customers.sql*
>
> *cs.baylor.edu/~speegle/pockjdbc/titles.sql*
>
> *cs.baylor.edu/~speegle/pockjdbc/tapes.sql*
>
> *cs.baylor.edu/~speegle/pockjdbc/orders.sql*

Use these files to load any database with the information needed for the program examples. Unfortunately, since the use of binary data is not consistent across databases, neither the Microsoft Access database nor the sql files contains the information needed to load the pictures used in the Titles table. The images are available on the Web site in the directory *cs.baylor.edu/~speegle/pockjdbc/images*, with each file named as in the *URL* field in the Titles table. By following the instructions of your local database, you should be able to load the image data into the database.

1.4 Analogy Continued

With a database installed and a class to handle connections, the next step is to exchange information between the database and a Java program. A *Statement* object is used to send SQL requests to the database. The SQL request can be a query (a Select statement) or an update (any of Insert, Update, or Delete statements). Likewise, a *Statement* object can send requests to modify the database schema, such as Create, Alter, or Drop statements. If the SQL request changes the database in any way, the *executeUpdate( )* method must be used. On the other hand, if the SQL request is a query, then the *executeQuery( )* method should be used. For example,

```
stmt.executeUpdate(
    "Insert into Customers values (999,'Greg Speegle','My House','My phone')");
stmt.executeQuery("Select Title, Price from Titles");
```

The *executeUpdate( )* method returns an integer telling us how many rows were updated (in the example, it would be 1). For database-altering requests—such as creating a table—the value returned is 0, since no rows are updated. The *executeQuery( )* method returns another member of the java.sql package, called the *ResultSet*.

In our analogy, the factory starts work on our order and produces the products we need. In JDBC, the *Statement* object sends the SQL query to the database, and the database produces the rows satisfying our query. These rows are collected into an object that satisfies the *ResultSet* interface. This *ResultSet* object corresponds to a truck being sent from the factory to the store. Notice that trucks are much larger than cars, just as *ResultSets* are much larger, in terms of system resources required, than *Statements* (see Figure 1.3).

The *ResultSet* interface is one of the largest in the java.sql package. In our analogy, many of the *ResultSet* methods correspond to unloading the truck at the store. A truck contains many boxes that must be unloaded one at a time. Then, each box has to be opened in order for its contents to be removed. *ResultSets* are treated in the same way. We must first find a row, then remove the contents of that row.

Fortunately, finding a row in a *ResultSet* is much easier than getting a forklift to a truck. The *ResultSet* object has a *cursor* indicating the current row. Before any rows have been "unloaded," the cursor references the nonexistent row before the first one. Once all of the rows have been "unloaded," the cursor references the nonexistent row after the last one. In order to change the position of the cursor, the method *next( )* is called. The *next( )* method will return *true* if the cursor currently references a valid row, and *false* otherwise.

So, if the *ResultSet* object is called *rs*, then the code to loop over all of the rows in *rs* would be

```
while (rs.next()) { do something }
```

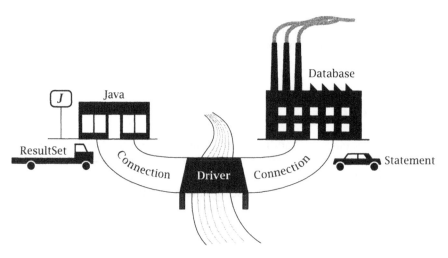

Figure 1.3: Analogy with *Statements* and *ResultSets*.

Under JDBC 1.0, we have to process each row of the *ResultSet* in order, from first to last. We cannot back up, nor can we skip ahead. These restrictions are relaxed in JDBC 2.0, and we explore the additional capabilities in Sections 2.3 and 4.3. Likewise, since it is required by some driver/database combinations, it is a good idea to process the columns in the row in order from left to right.

In order to process any of the columns, we have to use special methods from the *ResultSet* class. Inside each row, there are two items: the title, which is a string, and the price, which is a double. In order to access the string in the row, we use the *getString()* method, and correspondingly, we use the *getDouble()* method to get the double. A natural concern is the number of special get methods required by the *ResultSet* interface, since each seems to be used for a special case. These worries are somewhat justified, as the online API has 22 such methods, although some have been deprecated.

There are two last points. First, the special get methods as a whole are referenced as *getXXX()* methods. Second, each method takes either a string or an integer as a parameter. That's like reading the label on the products in the boxes from our truck. The string is the name of the desired column in the query, and the integer is the position (starting with 1) of the desired column. So, to print out one line for each row in the *ResultSet rs,* the code would be

```
while (rs.next())
      { System.out.println("The title is " + rs.getString("Title")
                  + " and it costs " + rs.getDouble(2)); }
```

Of course, within a particular example, the actual structure of the loop is often different. Now we look at an example to see how these pieces fit together to solve a simple problem.

1.5 Simple Example

Our first complete example accepts a customer ID and returns the title and type (DVD or VHS) of all tapes currently checked out by the customer. It is in the class SimpleJDBC. Although this class is very simple, this basic structure can be used to perform many simple queries on different databases. SimpleJDBC uses the default JDBC-ODBC bridge provided in the SDK via the class ConnectionJDBC (see Section 1.2). ConnectionJDBC can be modified to use any driver/database combination as the default. Consult the documentation for the specific driver for the strings needed.

SimpleJDBC.java

```
1    import java.sql.*;
2
3    public class SimpleJDBC extends ConnectionJDBC {
4        public static void main(String args[]) {
5            if (args.length != 1) {
6                System.out.println("Usage: java SimpleJDBC custid");
7                System.exit(1);
8            }
9
10           String query = "Select Title, Type " +
11               "from Orders O, Titles T, Tapes V " +
12               "where V.TapeId=O.TapeId and T.TitleId=V.TitleId and " +
13               "Status = '0' and " +
14               "O.CustomerID= " + args[0];
15
16           SimpleJDBC J = new SimpleJDBC();
17           Connection dbConnect = null;
18           Statement dbStatement = null;
19           ResultSet dbRS = null;
20           try {
21               dbConnect = J.makeConnection(); //from ConnectionJDBC
22               dbStatement = dbConnect.createStatement();
23               dbRS = dbStatement.executeQuery(query);
24               J.presentResultSet(dbRS);
25           } catch (SQLException sqlex) {
26               System.out.println(sqlex.getMessage());
27           } finally {
28               J.closeConnection(dbConnect,dbStatement); //from ConnectionJDBC
29           }
30       }
31
32       public void presentResultSet(ResultSet rs)
33           throws SQLException {
34           if (!rs.next()) System.out.println("No records for customer");
```

```
35              else {
36                  do {
37                      System.out.println(rs.getString("Title") + ": " +
38                                      rs.getString("Type"));
39                  } while (rs.next());
40              }
41      }
42  }
```

SimpleJDBC.java

SimpleJDBC inherits the makeConnection( ) and closeConnection( ) methods of Connection-JDBC. It also adds one additional method, presentResultSet( ). The main( ) method in lines 4–30 follows a pattern that is common in JDBC programs. First, the parameters are read and any errors are detected (lines 5–8). Next, a string containing the query is built (lines 10–14). Line 14 places the input parameter to the program, the customer ID, into the SQL query. This reduces the requirements on the user from entering an SQL query to typing the command

```
java SimpleJDBC 999
```

to find the movies currently checked out by the customer with ID 999. After the query is built, a SimpleJDBC object is created (line 16), and *Connection, Statement,* and *ResultSet* objects are declared (lines 17–19). We are now ready to connect our program to the database.

All of the JDBC part of the program is inside a try block since it can throw *SQLExceptions.* The first step is to make a connection by using the makeConnection( ) method in Connection-JDBC (see Section 1.2). Next, line 22 creates the *Statement* object. Line 23 creates a *ResultSet* object by executing the query defined in lines 10–14. In order to process the *ResultSet,* it is passed to the new method in this class. Any exceptions generate an error message, and lines 25–26 catch these exceptions. We always close the connection to the database, in this example with lines 27–29.

The presentResultSet( ) method in lines 32–41 simply displays all of the contents of a *ResultSet* on the screen. It accepts a *ResultSet* object as a parameter and throws any *SQLExceptions* generated back to the calling method. If there are no rows in the *ResultSet,* then the call to *next( )* in line 34 will fail and we output a simple message. If there are rows to be processed, the loop in lines 36–39 will access each row until there are no more rows left (at which time the call to *next* in line 39 will return *false).* For each line, the value in the title field is retrieved by the first call to *getString( )* (line 37) and the value of the type field is found by the second call in line 38.

SimpleJDBC can be modified to perform many simple operations on a database. The only parts that need to be changed are

- The code to check for command line arguments in lines 5–8

- The SQL query in lines 10–14

- The output string in lines 37–38

The rest of the program can remain exactly the same.

1.6 API Summary

The examples in this chapter use the basic classes and interfaces for connecting a Java program to a database. The most important methods are

- *Class.forName(String DriverName)*
- *DriverManager*
  - *getConnection(String Driver, String DatabaseURL)*
  - *getConnection(String Driver, String DatabaseURL, String Username, String Password)*
- *Connection*
  - *createStatement( )*
- *Statement*
  - *executeQuery(String SQLQuery)*
- *ResultSet*
  - *getXXX(String SQLQueryColumnName)*
  - *getXXX(int SQLQueryColumnNumber)*
  - *next( )*

1.7 Going Beyond

1. Modify SimpleJDBC.java so that it will continue to accept values until an invalid customer ID is entered. For each customer ID, the program will display the titles checked out.

2. Modify SimpleJDBC.java to output the name, address, and phone number of all customers with a tape checked out.

3. Modify SimpleJDBC.java to output the name of all customers who have ever checked out a tape of a certain title (input the title ID number).

4. One of the biggest challenges facing newcomers to JDBC is making an initial connection to a database. The program ConnectionJDBC is set up to allow many types of tests for making connections to a database. Intentionally input errors to the ConnectionJDBC and note the responses from the program. Some possible errors are

   - No driver loaded when making a connection
   - Invalid username and/or password
   - Invalid database URL

5. SimpleJDBC.java uses only one *Statement* per *Connection*. Some database systems can handle several *Statements* per *Connection*. Modify SimpleJDBC.java so that it has a second open *Statement* on the same *Connection*. Note the response to your queries when you

   a. Process all of one *ResultSet* before making the second *Statement*

b. Process all of one *ResultSet* after making the second *Statement* but before executing a query on it

c. Process all of one *ResultSet* after executing the query, but before retrieving any rows from the second *ResultSet*

d. Interleave processing of the *ResultSets* by selecting one row of each *ResultSet* inside the same loop

chapter 2

Presenting Information to Users

The first part of the JDBC puzzle we investigate in detail is presenting information to users. As we saw in the analogy in Sections 1.1 and 1.4, within JDBC, objects satisfying the *ResultSet* interface are returned to the user in response to queries. In the example of Section 1.5, the data in the *ResultSet* is simply printed to the screen. In today's world of interactive programs, a textual interface is unappealing and inefficient for users. In order to naturally present tabular information stored in databases with Java, we need a graphic component that resembles the table structure of databases.

The graphical component of choice is the *JTable* class in the javax.swing package. A database table contains rows, with each row comprised of columns. Within JDBC, the table resulting from a query is mapped to a *ResultSet* object. The example in Section 1.5 shows that in a *ResultSet* object, the cursor points to a particular row, and each field can be retrieved by specific operations, maintaining the "row and column" feel of the underlying database table. A *ResultSet* object can be translated into a *Vector* of *Vectors*. Each row in the ResultSet is turned into a *Vector* by adding all of the fields to a vector. Then all of the row *Vectors* can be added to another *Vector*. Finally, *JTable* objects have rows, each of which is mapped to a row *Vector*. The columns in the select clause of the query become the columns in the *JTable,* and all of the rows in the database satisfying the Where clause appear as rows in the JTable.

2.1 JTables

The use of *JTables* to represent relational database tables is very natural. Several third-party extensions to the *JTable* class automatically make this connection. Check the guide's web site for the latest listing of available classes. However, since this extension is not part of the API, we'll build our own so that we will know how these extended classes work.

Within the *JTable* class, there are two ways to construct an instance from a relational database table. Our first example uses the most straightforward approach, while Sections 2.2 and 2.3 present a more sophisticated approach. The basic technique takes a pair of vectors, one representing the headings for the database table and the other representing the data from the result set, and automatically builds a table from them. For example,

```
JTable dataTable = new JTable(dataVector, headVector);
```

creates a *JTable* with the headings from headVector and the data from dataVector. The parameter dataVector must be a *Vector* of *Vectors*. The resulting *JTable* will have one column for each object in headVector, and one row for each *Vector* in dataVector. Note that the number of objects within each subvector of dataVector must be the same as the number of objects in the headVector. If headVector has fewer elements than the subvector, then the excess columns will not be displayed in dataTable. If the headVector has more elements than the subvectors, an *ArrayIndexOutofBounds* exception is thrown when dataTable tries to access nonexistent elements.

The only problem that remains is that relational database tables can be much larger than what we can show on a screen at one time. This problem is commonly solved by placing the *JTable* inside of another swing object, the *JScrollPane*. Once again, we have two choices on how to put the *JTable* inside the *JScrollPane*: 1) use the *JScrollPane* constructor, which takes a *Component* as a parameter; or 2) use the *setViewportView(C)* method, which puts *Component* C into the viewable portion of the *JScrollPane*. In general, using the *ViewportView( )* method is preferred, since it does not create additional objects.

The program example, JTableJDBC, shows how *JTables* can display data. It performs the same task as SimpleJDBC—displaying the tapes currently checked out to a user. The only difference is that we are using a graphic user interface (GUI) instead of command line arguments. It uses packages other than java.sql, specifically javax.swing (for *JTable* methods), java.awt.event (for event handling), and java.util (for *Vector* methods). All of these additional methods are required for this program to use a GUI to display the database results. JTableJDBC also extends the Java class GUIJDBC, which is not presented here (see the Appendix). GUIJDBC defines four GUI components of interest: inputText, inputButton, inputLabel, and the BorderLayout for the window. These components are needed for the completeness of the program, but they do not have any JDBC implications, so no further discussion is presented in this book.

JTableJDBC

```
 1  import java.sql.*;
 2  import javax.swing.*;
 3  import java.awt.event.*;
 4  import java.util.*;
 5
 6  public class JTableJDBC extends GUIJDBC {
 7      JTable dataTable = new JTable();
 8      JScrollPane dataTableScrollPane = new JScrollPane();
 9
10      public static void main(String args[]) {
11          JTableJDBC jtJDBC = new JTableJDBC("JDBC Program with JTables");
12          jtJDBC.show();
```

```
13          jtJDBC.pack();
14      }
15
16      public JTableJDBC(String title) {
17          super(title);
18          dataTableScrollPane.setViewportView(dataTable);
19          getContentPane().add("Center",dataTableScrollPane);//from GUIJDBC
20      }
21
22      public void actionPerformed(ActionEvent evt) {
23          String query = "Select Title, Type " +
24              "from Orders O, Titles T, Tapes V " +
25              "where V.TapeId=O.TapeId and T.TitleId=V.TitleId and " +
26              "Status = 'O' and " +
27              "O.CustomerID= " + inputText.getText().trim();
28
29          ConnectionJDBC CJ = new ConnectionJDBC(); //from ConnectionJDBC
30          Connection dbConnect = null;
31          Statement dbStatement = null;
32          ResultSet dbRS = null;
33          try {
34              dbConnect = CJ.makeConnection(); //from ConnectionJDBC
35              dbStatement = dbConnect.createStatement();
36              dbRS = dbStatement.executeQuery(query);
37              presentResultSet(dbRS);
38          } catch (SQLException sqlex) {
39              JOptionPane.showMessageDialog(null,sqlex.getMessage());
40          }
41          finally {
42              CJ.closeConnection(dbConnect,dbStatement);
43          }
44      }
45
46      public void presentResultSet(ResultSet rs)
47          throws SQLException {
48          Vector dataVector = new Vector();
49          if (!rs.next())
50              JOptionPane.showMessageDialog(null,"No records for customer");
51          else {
52              do {
53                  Vector rowVector = new Vector();
54                  rowVector.addElement(rs.getString("Title"));
55                  rowVector.addElement(rs.getString("Type"));
56                  dataVector.addElement(rowVector);
57                  } while (rs.next());
58          }
59          Vector headVector = new Vector(2);
```

```
60        headVector.addElement("Title");
61        headVector.addElement("Type");
62        dataTable = new JTable(dataVector, headVector);
63        dataTableScrollPane.setViewportView(dataTable);
64    }
65  }
```

JTableJDBC

Line 7 of JTableJDBC defines a new *JTable* object called dataTable, and line 8 declares the *JScrollPane* object called dataTableScrollPane. These two GUI components will be used in all of the GUI applications in this guide.

Lines 10-14 are a simple main method for the class. All it does is create an instance of the JTableJDBC class and display it to the screen. The parameter to the constructor is the title to be displayed on the window.

The constructor for the class is in lines 16-20. The first step is to call the constructor for GUIJDBC. This creates all of the components for the interface and sets up this object as a "listener" for events, such as the user clicking a button or closing the window. The next step is to place dataTable inside the *JScrollPane*, so that lengthy responses can still be displayed to the user. Line 18 does just that. Finally, line 19 places the dataTableScrollPane in the center of the *ContentPane*, which is the window created for the program. Note that the dataTable is still empty when the constructor completes, therefore the window for the program contains only the input components from GUIJDBC.

Whenever the user clicks on the "query" button or hits "enter" while the text field is active, the *actionPerformed( )* method is called for all programs listening for that event. In this case, the JTableJDBC class inherits listening from GUIJDBC. In this method, we perform all of the database access steps that are in SimpleJDBC. In lines 23-27 we see the exact same query as before, except that we are getting the Customer ID number from the *JTextField* object inputText instead of from the command line.

Line 29 creates a ConnectionJDBC object using the default constructor. Lines 30-32 declare the *Connection, Statement,* and *ResultSet* objects that we always need to query a database. Hopefully, lines 33-43 look familiar, as they are almost identical to lines 30-40 in SimpleJDBC. The biggest difference is line 39. Since JTableJDBC uses a GUI, error messages should be displayed on the screen instead of to a command prompt. The *JOptionPane* method *showMessageDialog( )* accepts a string to be displayed on the user's screen. If the first parameter is *null* (as in this case) the message is displayed in a default frame. The only other differences are related to object names. However, although the presentResultSet( ) method is called in both classes, it is implemented differently here.

The presentResultSet( ) method is in lines 46-64. In order to display data retrieved in a *ResultSet* object in a *JTable*, we have to convert the data into a pair of *Vectors*. The first *Vector* contains the data, so it is called the *dataVector*. The second *Vector* contains the headings for the *JTable*, so it is called the *headVector*. The dataVector must be a *Vector* of *Vectors*, where each subvector contains one row to be displayed on the screen. The simplest path is to display a row from the *ResultSet* as a row in the *JTable*.

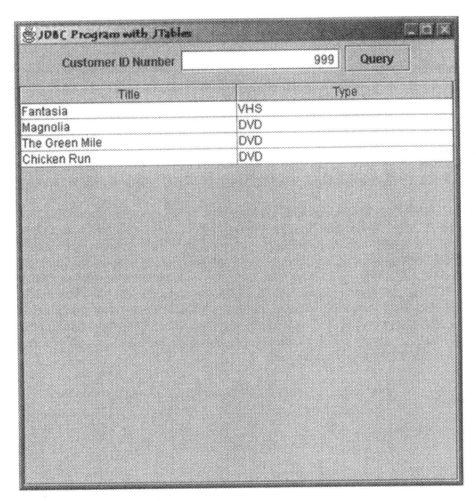

Figure 2.1: *JTable* interface after query.

Lines 52–58 make this conversion. A *Vector* (called *rowVector*) is created, and the attribute values from the *ResultSet* are added to rowVector. In line 56, rowVector is added to dataVector. Thus, dataVector becomes a *Vector* of *Vectors*. The same do-while loop structure of SimpleJDBC is used to process all of the rows in the *ResultSet*. Once the loop exits, we need to construct the headings vector. In lines 59–61, we create the object and add the title elements.

Line 62 creates a new *JTable* object, but this time it uses the dataVector and the headVector we created. As a result, the data from the query is now part of the *JTable*. Line 63 sets the dataTable as the viewable portion of dataTableScrollPane. This causes the *JScrollPane* object to be updated as quickly as possible. A screen shot example of a user with several videos checked out is in Figure 2.1. Finally, note that line 50 outputs a simple message to the screen if the customer does not have any videos checked out.

2.2   *JTable* Example with *AbstractTableModel*

The simple approach in Section 2.1 works very well, as long as the information is entirely alphanumeric and the number of results returned from the query is not very large. However, if either of these cases are possible, we need more control over the *JTable*. To get this control, we need to understand more about how *JTables* work. The appearance of a *JTable* is controlled by the *TableModel* interface. This interface includes methods to set the number of columns and rows in the table and to determine the value and class of each element in the table. Fortunately, the *AbstractTableModel* class implements most of the *TableModel* interface. We create desired *TableModel* classes by extending the *AbstractTableModel* class and changing the interesting methods.

There are three methods we must always implement when we extend the *AbstractTable-Model*: *getRowCount( )*, *getColumnCount( )*, and *getValueAt(row, column)*. The method *getRow-Count( )* returns the number of rows in the table, while *getColumnCount( )* returns the number of columns, and the *getValueAt( )* method returns the actual object to be displayed at a particular row and column. The actual code for each of these methods depends on the underlying data representation. The example for this technique requires two classes. The TableModelJDBC class retrieves values from the user and submits the query to the database. The second class, JDBCTableModel, uses a *Vector* of *Vectors* approach to represent the data in the *JTable*. In this example, JDBCTableModel is very simple in order to demonstrate the basic structure of this type of GUI. We discuss the table model part first.

JDBCTableModel

```
1    import javax.swing.table.*;
2    import java.util.*;
3
4    public class JDBCTableModel extends AbstractTableModel {
5        Vector headVector = new Vector();
6        Vector dataVector = new Vector();
7
8        public void setHeading(Vector heading) { headVector = heading; }
9        public void setData(Vector data) { dataVector = data;}
10
11       public int getRowCount() { return dataVector.size(); }
12       public int getColumnCount() { return headVector.size(); }
13
14       public Object getValueAt(int rowIndex, int columnIndex) {
15           Object o = null;
16           if (rowIndex < dataVector.size()) {
17               Vector row = (Vector)dataVector.elementAt(rowIndex);
18               if (columnIndex < row.size()) {
19                   o = row.elementAt(columnIndex);
20               }
21           }
```

```
22          return 0;
23      }
24
25      public String getColumnName(int columnIndex) {
26          if (columnIndex < headVector.size()) {
27              return (String)headVector.elementAt(columnIndex);
28          } else { return new String("Unknown"); }
29      }
30  }
```

JDBCTableModel

The JDBCTableModel class does not use any database-related features, so it does not have to import the java.sql package. It does require the javax.swing.table package, so that it can extend the *AbstractTableModel* class (line 4) as well as the java.util package in order to use *Vectors*. Note also that JDBCTableModel works fine with the default constructor.

JDBCTableModel does add two data items to the *AbstractTableModel* class, headVector for the headings and dataVector for the data to be displayed in the table. Line 8 receives a *Vector* with the headings for the *JTable*, and line 9 receives the data to be passed in as well. As in JTableJDBC, the dataVector must be a *Vector* of *Vectors* and the size of the subvectors must match the size of the headVector.

The getRowCount( ) method in line 11 is one of the required methods for a class to extend the *AbstractTableModel*. Our method simply returns the number of rows (*Vectors*) in dataVector. Likewise, the getColumnCount( ) method (also required) returns the number of elements in the headVector. This binds our *JTable* to the size of the *Vectors* passed in.

Lines 14-23 define the last required method for a subclass of *AbstractTableModel*, specifically getValueAt( ). The getValueAt( ) method requires two parameters: the row and the column to be displayed. The parameter rowIndex is used to determine which element of dataVector should be used to find the data (line 17). Then, within that *Vector*, the columnIndex parameter determines the field to be returned. The getValueAt( ) method returns an *Object*. Since that is also returned by the *Vector* method *elementAt( )*, we can simply return that value. If no value in the dataVector corresponds to the requested location, then *null* is returned.

By default, the *AbstractTableModel* uses the spreadsheet style to label columns. That means that the first 26 columns have a single letter heading, beginning with *A*, then *B*, and so on. Once all of the single letters have been used, two-letter combinations are used. This default behavior is not desired in this case, since we know the titles for the columns. As such, we override the method for naming columns, getColumnName( ) in lines 25-29. This method accepts one parameter, the columnIndex, and returns a *String*. In our case, we simply return the corresponding element in the headVector.

With the JDBCTableModel defined, the requirements of a program to use it to display database information should be clear. In fact, the program should look a lot like the program JTableJDBC. Therefore, we begin with that program and extend it to handle our new *TableModel*.

TableModelJDBC

```
1   import java.sql.*;
2   import javax.swing.*;
3   import javax.swing.table.*;
4   import java.awt.event.*;
5   import java.util.*;
6
7   public class TableModelJDBC extends JTableJDBC {
8       JDBCTableModel jtm = null;
9
10      public static void main(String args[]) {
11          TableModelJDBC tmJDBC = new TableModelJDBC("JDBC w/Table Model");
12          tmJDBC.show();
13          tmJDBC.pack();
14      }
15
16      public TableModelJDBC(String title) {
17          super(title);
18          jtm = new JDBCTableModel();
19          Vector headVector = new Vector(2);
20          headVector.addElement("Title");
21          headVector.addElement("Type");
22          jtm.setHeading(headVector);
23          dataTable.setModel(jtm);
24      }
25
26      public void presentResultSet(ResultSet rs)
27          throws SQLException {
28          Vector dataVector = new Vector();
29          if (!rs.next())
30              JOptionPane.showMessageDialog(null,"No records for customer");
31          else {
32              do {
33                  Vector rowVector = new Vector();
34                  rowVector.addElement(rs.getString("Title"));
35                  rowVector.addElement(rs.getString("Type"));
36                  dataVector.addElement(rowVector);
37                  } while (rs.next());
38          }
39          jtm.setData(dataVector);
40          dataTableScrollPane.setViewportView(dataTable);//from JTableJDBC
41      }
42  }
```

TableModelJDBC imports exactly the same packages as JTableJDBC, and for exactly the same reasons. Likewise, it extends JTableJDBC, so that we can take advantage of the *JTable* and *JScrollPane* objects defined there, in addition to the GUI components defined in GUIJDBC. The new data member added by TableModelJDBC is the JDBCTableModel object jtm. The main method in lines 10-14 performs the same functionality as the main method for JTableJDBC.

The first real difference between the programs occurs at the constructor. In TableModelJDBC, we create the *Vector* for the headings here and pass it to jtm (lines 18-22). This way, headVector is only created once, instead of many times as in JTableJDBC (to see how this optimization is also possible for JTableJDBC, turn to Section 2.6). Also, in line 23, the *setModel* method provides a *JTable* object with a custom *TableModel* instead of the default (which is used in JTableJDBC). Since the headings are already set in jtm, when the window is displayed, the headings for the *JTable* will be in the frame.

In TableModelJDBC, there is no actionPerformed( ) method. This is because we can inherit the method from JTableJDBC, as there are no changes in the method at all. However, we do have to modify the presentResultSet( ) method, since we are using a different *TableModel*. The differences between the two programs are small. We output the same message if no customers are found. We perform exactly the same operations to convert the *ResultSet* into a *Vector* of *Vectors*. Then, in line 39, we call the setData( ) method of the JDBCTableModel to change the underlying data instead of creating a new *JTable* in JTableJDBC. We also do not have to create the heading *Vector*, since our custom *TableModel* allows us to set the headings once and use them repeatedly.

2.3   JDBC 2.0 *ResultSets*

Being forced to process a *ResultSet* from top to bottom (and sometimes from left to right as well) is not always desirable. In the JDBC 2.0 API, this restriction is removed by allowing more sophisticated *ResultSet* objects. We can access these *ResultSet* objects by creating more sophisticated *Statement* objects. The *createStatement( )* method in the *Connection* interface has another signature, this one with two parameters. The first parameter is the *resultSetType*, and the second is the *resultSetConcurrency*. Concurrency values are discussed in Section 4.3. The values for these two parameters appear in the *ResultSet* interface. The three possible values for the *resultSetType* are

1. TYPE_FORWARD_ONLY: This is the default *resultSetType*, and the *ResultSet* can only be processed from the first row to the last.

2. TYPE_SCROLL_INSENSITIVE: This *resultSetType* allows dynamic access to the rows, including jumping to any specific row in the *ResultSet*. The "INSENSITIVE" label means that the *ResultSet* will not see changes made by other users.

3. TYPE_SCROLL_SENSITIVE: This *resultSetType* not only allows dynamic access, but in addition the *ResultSet* can change as a result of modifications to the database by others. Such a *ResultSet* would be very useful in monitoring a dynamic situation, such as a stock price or inventory.

In order to dynamically move the cursor around a *ResultSet*, the key methods are *absolute( )* and *relative( )*. The *absolute( )* method takes an integer as a parameter and moves to that row. The rows are numbered starting with 1. The method returns *true* if the cursor is on a valid row, and *false* otherwise. For example, we could loop through a *ResultSet* rs by

```
i=1;
while (rs.absolute(i++)) { do something; }
```

We can also access rows from the end of the *ResultSet* by using negative integers. In this case, the last row is -1, the next-to-last -2, and so on. This means we can process a *ResultSet* rs backward by

```
i=-1;
while (rs.absolute(i--)) { do something; }
```

Passing in the value of 0 for the parameter results in an *SQLException*.

The *relative( )* method also accepts an integer as a parameter, and it moves the cursor the number of rows indicated. However, the *relative( )* method only works if the cursor currently points at a valid row. Otherwise, it throws an *SQLException*. For example,

```
rs.next();
while(rs.relative(1)) { do something; }
```

will loop through the *ResultSet* rs. Negative integers cause the cursor to move backward through the *ResultSet*. A value of 0 is legal but doesn't do anything.

The *ResultSet* interface also includes the methods *first( )* and *last( )*, which move the cursor to either the first or last row, respectively. Additionally, the interface contains the method *getRow( )*, which returns the row number. This provides an easy mechanism to determine the number of rows in the *ResultSet*,

```
rs.last();
numberRows = rs.getRow();
```

Our program example for using JDBC 2.0 *ResultSet* objects replaces the use of vectors within our *JTable* example. The program consists of two new parts: JDBC2TableModel, which extends JDBCTableModel, and TableModelJDBC2, which extends TableModelJDBC. As with the example in Section 2.2, we begin with the *TableModel* class.

JDBC2TableModel

```
1   import java.sql.*;
2
3   public class JDBC2TableModel extends JDBCTableModel {
4       ConnectionJDBC CJ = null;
5       Connection dbConnect = null;
6       Statement dbStatement = null;
7       ResultSet dbRS = null;
8
```

```
9     public JDBC2TableModel() {
10        super();
11        CJ = new ConnectionJDBC();
12        try {
13            dbConnect =
14                CJ.makeConnection("oracle.jdbc.driver.OracleDriver",
15                            "jdbc:oracle:oci8:@","jdbc_user","guest");
16            dbStatement =
17                dbConnect.createStatement(ResultSet.TYPE_SCROLL_INSENSITIVE,
18                                ResultSet.CONCUR_READ_ONLY);
19        } catch (SQLException sqlex) {
20            System.out.println(sqlex.getMessage());
21        }
22    }
23
24    public void showQuery(String query) {
25        try {
26            dbRS = dbStatement.executeQuery(query);
27        } catch (SQLException sqlex) {System.out.println(sqlex.getMessage()); }
28    }
29
30    public int getRowCount() {
31        if (dbRS==null) return 0;
32        else {
33            try {
34                dbRS.last();
35                return dbRS.getRow();
36            } catch (SQLException sqlex) {return 0;}
37        }
38    }
39
40    public Object getValueAt(int rowIndex, int columnIndex) {
41        if (dbRS==null) return null;
42        try {
43            if (!dbRS.absolute(rowIndex+1)) return null;
44            return dbRS.getString(columnIndex+1);
45        } catch (SQLException sqlex) {return null;}
46    }
47
48    public void closeConnection() {
49        CJ.closeConnection(dbConnect, dbStatement);
50    }
51 }
```

JDBC2TableModel

The dynamic access possible with JDBC 2.0 allows us to use *ResultSet* objects instead of *Vectors* to format information for *JTable* objects. As such, we push all of the database access information into the *TableModel*. Therefore, this class requires the java.sql package, so that we can have access to *Connection, Statement,* and *ResultSet* objects. However, it also inherits all of the methods from JDBCTableModel. This allows us to determine the headings of the JTable by using *Vectors* and the setHeading( ) method of JDBCTableModel.

JDBC2TableModel contains four data members: a ConnectionJDBC object, a *Connection* object, a *Statement* object, and a *ResultSet* object. These are used throughout the class to determine the values to be presented in the *JTable.*

The first interesting piece of JDBC2TableModel is in lines 13–15. Here we create a *Connection* object, but instead of using the default parameters for the makeConnection( ) method, we pass in four parameters. These parameters are required for a connection to an Oracle database running on the local machine. (More information about these parameters is in Section 5.1.) We use the Oracle driver because the default JDBC-ODBC bridge with an Access ODBC data source does not support JDBC 2.0-style result sets.

Lines 16–18 create a sophisticated *Statement* object that supports scrolling but is not sensitive to changes by other transactions. The concurrency type is read only, which is fine since we are only generating reports. (For more detail on the meaning of this and other concurrency types, see Section 4.3.)

The method showQuery( ) in lines 24–28 is the interface between the calling program and a JDBC2TableModel instance. The method accepts a *String*, which should be an SQL query. The *Statement* dbStatement executes the query and generates dbRS, the *ResultSet* object for the *TableModel*. Since JDBC2TableModel extends *AbstractTableModel* (via JDBCTable-Model), it must define the three methods, *getRowCount( ), getColumnCount( ),* and *getValueAt( ).* JDBC2TableModel inherits the definition of JDBCTableModel for getColumnCount( ), because this example still uses the same method for setting the headings of the JTable. However, since there are different methods for determining the data to be presented, we have to override the definitions of the other two methods.

Lines 30–38 implement the getRowCount( ) method using the dynamic capabilities of *ResultSets*. In line 34, we go to the last row in the *ResultSet*, and line 35 returns the row number. Under many database/driver combinations, this is accomplished by reading all of the rows in the query, so this operation can be slow.

The getValueAt( ) method in lines 40–46 is also implemented using the JDBC 2.0 dynamic access capabilities. Line 43 advances the cursor to the *ResultSet* row that corresponds to the row in the JTable. The rowIndex parameter begins at 0 while the *ResultSet* object numbers rows starting with 1. So, we have to add 1 to the index to find the correct row. If there is no such row, the *absolute( )* method returns *false,* so the getValueAt( ) method returns *null.* If the row is valid, the *getString( )* method is called to retrieve the value from the current row. As with row numbering, the columns are also numbered inconsistently. We add 1 to the columnIndex parameter to find the corresponding column in the *ResultSet*. The getString( ) method works, because the database values returned by the query are VARCHAR and CHAR types. Likewise, other data types can be retrieved by this method, depending on the database/driver combination. However, the results displayed are better if appropriate methods are used.

Finally, there is no way for the JDBCTableModel class to know when the connection to the database is no longer needed. The closeConnection( ) method of lines 48–50 is used for the calling class to signal the end of execution. All this method does is call the closeConnection( ) method of the ConnectionJDBC class, but that ends the database connection.

Since JDBC2TableModel contains all of the interesting database code, it is not surprising that the interface program is very simple. The main program is very similar to JDBCTableModel, except that a TableModelJDBC2 object is created. Likewise, the only difference between the constructors of the two classes is that a JDBC2TableModel object is instantiated and used as the *TableModel* for the class. (In fact, the creation of the headVector in lines 19–21 could be skipped, because it is the same vector in JDBCTableModel.)

TableModelJDBC2

```
1   import java.util.*;
2   import java.awt.event.*;
3
4   public class TableModelJDBC2 extends TableModelJDBC {
5       JDBC2TableModel j2tm = null;
6
7       public static void main(String args[]) {
8           TableModelJDBC2 tmJDBC = new TableModelJDBC2("JDBC2.0 w/Table Model");
9           tmJDBC.show();
10          tmJDBC.pack();
11      }
12
13      public TableModelJDBC2(String title) {
14          super(title);
15          j2tm = new JDBC2TableModel();
16          Vector headVector = new Vector(2);
17          headVector.addElement("Title");
18          headVector.addElement("Type");
19          j2tm.setHeading(headVector);
20          dataTable.setModel(j2tm); //from JTableJDBC
21      }
22
23      public void actionPerformed(ActionEvent evt) {
24          String query = "Select Title, Type " +
25              "from Orders O, Titles T, Tapes V " +
26              "where V.TapeId=O.TapeId and T.TitleId=V.TitleId and " +
27              "Status = '0' and " +
28              "O.CustomerID= " + inputText.getText().trim();
29          j2tm.showQuery(query);
30          dataTableScrollPane.setViewportView(dataTable); //from JTableJDBC2
31      }
32
```

```
33   public void exitWindow(int i) {
34       j2tm.closeConnection();
35       System.exit(i);
36   }
37 }
```

The biggest difference between TableModelJDBC2 and TableModelJDBC is the actionPerformed( ) method. TableModelJDBC2 only has to pass the query (built in lines 24–28) to the JDBC2TableModel class (line 29), and then display the results (line 30). The only remaining method is exitWindow( ), which is called when the user closes the window (inherited from GUIJDBC). We change this method so that the closeConnection( ) method in JDBC2TableModel is called, signaling the end of the program execution.

2.4 Serializing *ResultSets*

One of the drawbacks to the *ResultSet* interface is that it does not implement the *Serializable* interface. From a technical standpoint, this is reasonable because *ResultSet* objects rely on several components, such as the connection to the database and the *Statement* object used to generate the *ResultSet*. In our analogy, there is no mechanism to airlift the truck to another location. It can only drive on the roads provided for it.

However, there are times when the information retrieved from a database needs to be transmitted to another program or saved as a file. Within Java, this is accomplished by serializing objects and using the *ObjectOutputStream* and the *ObjectInputStream*. Since *ResultSet* objects cannot be serialized, we have to convert the data into another format in order to transmit the information.

Fortunately for us, *Vectors* are serializable if all of the elements in them can be serialized. Thus, the transformation for *JTables* in Section 2.1 is also useful for serializing results. The program SerializedJDBC.java is an example of serializing the objects. It stores them as a file, but other uses are possible (such as sending them over sockets, as in Section 6.3.2).

SerializedJDBC

```
1  import java.sql.*;
2  import java.util.*;
3  import java.io.*;
4
5  public class SerializedJDBC extends ConnectionJDBC {
6      public static void main(String args[]) {
7          if (args.length != 1) {
8              System.out.println("Usage: java SerializedJDBC custid");
9              System.exit(1);
10         }
```

```
11
12       String query = "Select Title, Type " +
13           "from Orders O, Titles T, Tapes V " +
14           "where V.TapeId=O.TapeId and T.TitleId=V.TitleId and " +
15           "Status = '0' and " +
16           "O.CustomerID= " + args[0];
17
18       SerializedJDBC J = new SerializedJDBC();
19       Connection dbConnect = null;
20       Statement dbStatement = null;
21       ResultSet dbRS = null;
22       try {
23           dbConnect = J.makeConnection(); // from ConnectionJDBC
24           dbStatement = dbConnect.createStatement();
25           dbRS = dbStatement.executeQuery(query);
26           J.presentResultSet(dbRS);
27       } catch (Exception ex) {
28           System.out.println(ex.getMessage());
29       }
30       finally {
31           J.closeConnection(dbConnect,dbStatement); // from ConnectionJDBC
32       }
33   }
34
35   public void presentResultSet(ResultSet rs)
36       throws SQLException, IOException {
37       Vector dataVector = new Vector();
38       if (!rs.next()) System.out.println("No records for customer");
39       else {
40           do {
41               Vector rowVector = new Vector();
42               rowVector.addElement(rs.getString("Title"));
43               rowVector.addElement(rs.getString("Type"));
44               dataVector.addElement(rowVector);
45           } while (rs.next());
46       }
47       FileOutputStream fostream = new FileOutputStream("records.tmp");
48       ObjectOutputStream oos = new ObjectOutputStream(fostream);
49       oos.writeObject(dataVector);
50       oos.flush();
51       fostream.close();
52   }
53 }
```

Serialized JDBC

Since the program writes objects to a file, there is no need to inherit from GUIJDBC or to import the swing or awt packages. SerializedJDBC does import java.sql for the database connections, java.util for the *Vector* class, and java.io for the input and output streams. SerializedJDBC extends ConnectionJDBC to take care of the methods to connect to the database.

The main( ) method (lines 6-33) is identical to the main( ) method in SimpleJDBC, with the exception that in SerializedJDBC, a SerializedJDBC object is created instead of a SimpleJDBC object. The difference between the two classes is in the presentResultSet( ) method. However, the presentResultSet( ) method for SerializedJDBC is very similar to the presentResultSet( ) method in JTableJDBC. In both cases, we convert the *ResultSet* into a *Vector* of *Vectors* with a do-while loop (lines 40-45 in SerializedJDBC). Since the attributes in the database are simple strings, the *Vector* can be serialized. In order to do so, we first create a *FileOutputStream* object, called *fostream*, passing in the name of a file. In this example, we hard code the filename "records.tmp." An *ObjectOutputStream*, oos, is created from fostream. All that remains is to write the dataVector to oos, which is accomplished by the simple *writeObject( )* method in line 49. To complete saving the object to the file, we flush the output stream (line 50) and close the file (line 51).

2.5 API Summary

In this chapter, the class examples transformed information from *ResultSet* objects to Java Swing objects. The primary classes and methods for performing this transformation are

- *JTable*
  - *setModel(TableModel TableModelObject)*
  - *new JTable(Vector headings, Vector data)*
- *JScrollPane*
  - *setViewportView(Component dataTable)*
- *AbstractTableModel*
  - *getRowCount( )*
  - *getColumnCount( )*
  - *getValueAt(int rowIndex, int columnIndex)*
- *Connection*
  - *createStatement(ResultSetType ScrollingANDSensitivity, ResultSetConcurrency ReadOnlyORUpdatable)*
- *ResultSet*
  - *absolute(int i)*
  - *relative(int i)*

2.6 Going Beyond

1. JTableJDBC creates the same headings vector every time a *ResultSet* is to be displayed. Clearly, this can be improved. Modify JTableJDBC.java so that headVector is only constructed once.

2. JTableJDBC creates a connection to the database for every query. Clearly, this is inefficient, as connections are expensive operations. Thus, the program could run faster if a connection is made at the beginning and used for all operations. The problem with this approach is that the database may close a connection without telling the program. Modify JTableJDBC.java so that it uses only one connection. Then, determine the amount of time your database will allow before closing a connection. Hint: Database queries will fail with unusual errors if the connection is closed.

3. Write a program to retrieve the serialized objects stored in a file by SerializedJDBC.java.

4. Send a query to JDBC2TableModel such that the values returned by the database are not strings. What happens?

chapter **3**

Querying the Database

Whereas Chapter 2 contains some of the common ways to process *ResultSet* objects, this chapter looks at the different ways to query the database by creating different *Statement* objects. The *Statement* class is extended by two subclasses, *PreparedStatement* and *CallableStatement* (which is a subclass of *PreparedStatement*). *PreparedStatements* are used when a query or update is going to be repeated often. It generally has greater initial overhead than *Statement* objects, but has better performance in future executions. The *CallableStatement* interface is used to execute stored procedures on the database. Both *PreparedStatements* and *CallableStatements* can generate dynamic and updatable *ResultSets*, as in Section 2.3.

3.1 *PreparedStatements*

Recall from our analogy that after the road is built from our store to the factory, the "statement car" drives the SQL order to the factory. The factory then processes the order and ships the products to our store. If the factory could begin work on our order sooner, the order would be filled quicker. Unfortunately, we usually don't know the entire order beforehand, but we might know some parts of it. For example, we might know that we want green gadgets, but we don't know if we want blue handles or red handles. If the statement car left early and told the factory we wanted green gadgets, but to hold off on the handles, the factory could begin work on the gadgets. When we know if we want red handles or blue handles, another statement car can be sent with that information. Ideally, the factory should then be able to produce the product quicker.

This is exactly the idea behind the *PreparedStatement* interface. When a *PreparedStatement* is created, part of the query is sent to the database. The query must include the tables used in the query and the names of the columns returned (in other words, the Select and From clauses). However, parts of the Where clause can be omitted, with the understanding that they will be filled in later.

The ability to do part of the query ahead of time is very beneficial when large numbers of similar queries are going to be sent to the database. A typical database management system

(DBMS) will cache the information about the query and thus perform subsequent queries faster than if each query were sent individually.

In order for the database to begin work on the query early, the *PreparedStatement* object is created with part of the query already provided. For example, if our previous programs used *PreparedStatements*, the *PreparedStatement* object pStmt would be created by

```
pStmt = dbConnect.prepareStatement("Select Title, Type
        From Orders O, Tapes V, Titles T
    Where V.TapeId=O.TapeId and Status = 'O' and
        T.TitleId=V.TitleId and O.CustomerID= ?"
```

The question mark in the SQL query is the placeholder. Once the user inputs the customer's ID, we can set the placeholder to the correct value by various *setXXX()* methods, such as

```
pStmt.setInt(1,custId);
```

Just as *ResultSets* have *getXXX()* methods to retrieve different values, *PreparedStatements* have setXXX() methods. The correct method must be used to match the type of the expected value. We also have to be careful with the index of the setXXX() method. The compiler will not catch the error of trying to set a value for a nonexistent placeholder. That is because the placeholder appears in a string that is being passed to the database. Therefore, we must test *PreparedStatements* thoroughly to make sure we are using them correctly.

After all placeholders have been set to a value, a *PreparedStatement* is executed by the simple method

```
pStmt.executeQuery();
```

Although *PreparedStatements* are subclasses of *Statements*, and therefore the *executeQuery()* method could be passed a string, it is a poor programming practice and should be avoided. In many database/driver combinations, it will generate an exception.

The program example for using *PreparedStatements* is PreparedJDBC.java. It extends the JTableJDBC class by replacing *Statement* objects with *PreparedStatement* objects.

PreparedJDBC

```
 1  import java.sql.*;
 2  import javax.swing.*;
 3  import java.awt.event.*;
 4
 5  public class PreparedJDBC extends JTableJDBC {
 6      ConnectionJDBC CJ = null;
 7      Connection dbConnect = null;
 8      PreparedStatement dbStatement = null;
 9
10      public static void main(String args[]) {
11          PreparedJDBC PJ = new PreparedJDBC("PreparedStatement Example");
12          PJ.show();
13          PJ.pack();
14      }
```

```
15
16      public PreparedJDBC(String text) {
17          super(text);
18          try {
19              CJ = new ConnectionJDBC();
20              dbConnect = CJ.makeConnection();
21              dbStatement = dbConnect.prepareStatement
22                  ("Select Title, Type " +
23                   "From Orders O, Titles T, Tapes V " +
24                   "Where V.TapeId=O.TapeId and T.TitleId=V.TitleId and " +
25                   "Status = 'O' and O.CustomerID = ?");
26          } catch (SQLException sqlex) {
27              JOptionPane.showMessageDialog(null,sqlex.getMessage());
28          }
29      }
30
31      public void actionPerformed(ActionEvent evt) {
32          int custId = Integer.parseInt(inputText.getText().trim());//in GUIJDBC
33          ResultSet dbRS = null;
34          try {
35              dbStatement.setInt(1,custId);
36              dbRS = dbStatement.executeQuery();
37              presentResultSet(dbRS); //from JTableJDBC
38          } catch (SQLException sqlex) {
39              System.out.println(sqlex.getMessage());
40          }
41      }
42
43      public void exitWindow(int i) {
44          CJ.closeConnection(dbConnect,dbStatement);
45          System.exit(i);
46      }
47  }
```

PreparedJDBC

The first difference between PreparedJDBC and JTableJDBC is the placement of the JDBC components. In Section 2.1, the JDBC objects are created whenever a user makes a request. In PreparedJDBC, the JDBC objects are data members (lines 6–8). We make this change because *PreparedStatements* should be executed many times. If not, then *Statement* objects are usually more efficient. Therefore, we assume that the user will make many database requests in a relatively short amount of time. Thus, we do not want to re-create the objects and lose the advantage of *PreparedStatements*.

This change motivates the next difference between the two programs, specifically, the constructor in lines 16–29. The JTableJDBC constructor does nothing besides use the GUI-JDBC constructor to set up the GUI. Since PreparedJDBC has JDBC object data members, the constructor is used to define their values. Line 19 creates a new ConnctionJDBC object, then line 20 uses that object to create a default connection for dbConnect. Lines 21-25 create the *PreparedStatement* object with the same SQL query as in our other examples. *PreparedStatements* use placeholders (the question mark at the end of the string) to receive data input by the user.

The actionPerformed( ) method in lines 31-41 is also slightly different. First, the *String* object returned by the inputText.getText( ) method should be converted into an integer, since the field in the database is an integer. The method *setInt( )* in line 35 then applies the value entered by the user to the placeholder in the *PreparedStatement* object. The first parameter indicates which placeholder will be assigned the value. Line 36 executes the query, with no parameter passed to it. Finally, line 37 presents the *ResultSet* using the method found in the JTableJDBC class.

Lines 43-46 close the connection to the database when the program exits. It simply calls the closeConnection( ) method of ConnectionJDBC. Since *PreparedStatements* are subclasses of *Statements,* we can pass dbStatement to the method without a problem.

3.2 *CallableStatements*

The *CallableStatement* interface executes a stored procedure at the DBMS. In order to explain how the interface works, I will first present an example of a stored procedure. Unlike the previous examples, the stored procedure does not show all of the tapes checked out to a customer, but instead tells us which customer has checked out a tape. The reason for the change is that stored procedures return values in two different ways: the first is via output parameters, as in this example; the second is as a *ResultSet* in a return value. This second mechanism requires database-specific routines to access the *ResultSet,* so it is beyond the scope of this guide. The language for the stored procedure is Procedural Language/Structured Query Language (PL/SQL). This simple example defines parameters and local variables (as a typical structured programming procedure does), then performs an SQL query. The results are processed by cursors, which are very similar to *ResultSet* objects in JDBC.

Stored Procedure customer_has

```
1   create or replace procedure customer_has
2        (tape_in IN integer,
3         name_out OUT Customers.CustomerName%type,
4         phone_out OUT Customers.CustomerPhone%type) as
5   cursor c1 is
6   Select CustomerName, CustomerPhone
7   From Customers, Tapes, Orders
8   Where Status = '0' and Orders.TapeId=Tapes.Tapeid
9   and Orders.CustomerId = Customers.CustomerId and
10  Tapes.TapeId = tape_in;
11
```

```
12  begin
13  open c1;
14  fetch c1 into name_out, phone_out;
15  if c1%NOTFOUND then name_out :='Available'; phone_out := '000';
16  END if;
17  close c1;
18  end customer_has;
```

Stored Procedure customer_has

Line 1 saves the procedure, named "customer_has," into the database, making it available for use. If a procedure with the same name is already in the database, the "or replace" clause will remove the old copy from the database. The only input parameter into the procedure is the tape ID. The two output parameters are the customer's name and phone number. The syntax in line 3 declares name_out to be the same type as the CustomerName attribute in the Customers table. Likewise, phone_out is declared to be the same type as the CustomerPhone attribute.

Lines 6-9 define a parameterized query, similar to how we have parameterized queries within *Statement* objects. The parameter tape_in is used to supply the value for the query. Line 5 declares a "cursor," which corresponds to a *ResultSet* object in JDBC.

The execution of the stored procedure is in lines 12-18. We first open the cursor and then "fetch" a row into the output parameters. The first field in the query is placed into the first value (in this case, name_out), and the second field is placed into phone_out. Line 15 takes advantage of the programming language part of PL/SQL by using a branching statement, not a part of SQL. If no customer has checked out the tape, the fetch command of line 14 will set an error flag. The %notfound predicate tests this error flag and returns *true* if it is set. If the query results are empty, then we indicate it by setting name_out to "Available" and phone_out to a nonsense value, "000." The END IF construct in line 16 terminates the if statement, and the cursor is closed in line 17.

Within JDBC, we can access this stored procedure by using the *CallableStatement* interface. *CallableStatement* is a subclass of *PreparedStatement* and has a similar form. A *CallableStatement* object is created by the *Connection* method *prepareCall()*. The *prepareCall()* method accepts a highly structured string as a parameter. For example, in order to use the customer_has procedure with the *CallableStatement* object hasTape,

```
CallableStatement hasTape = dbConnect.prepareCall("{call customer_has(?,?,?)}");
```

The string begins and ends with { and }, respectively. The braces indicate that the string should be translated into the native syntax for the DBMS. Actually, the braces can be used in any database string, but if they are not needed, they should not be used since they consume extra resources. However, in this case they are needed, since the language for stored procedures is not the same on different databases.

The "call" in the string is a keyword and must be part of a *prepareCall* statement. The procedure name and a formal parameter list follow the "call" keyword. There are different statements to assign actual parameters to the placeholders depending on the type of the parameter. An IN parameter can be set much like a placeholder in a *PreparedStatement*, like this:

```
hasTape.setInt(1,27);
```

Of course, the constant 27 can be replaced with a variable as needed.

An OUT parameter requires a two-step process. The first step is to connect the Java program with the placeholder. This is done with the *registerOutParameter( )* method of the *CallableStatement* interface. This method takes two parameters: the first is the placeholder of the corresponding OUT parameter, and the second is the SQL type of the parameter. Continuing with the hasTape example,

```
hasTape.registerOutParameter(2,Types.INTEGER);
```

Notice that the SQL type is *Types.INTEGER*. This is referencing the *java.sql.Types* class. Within that class are all of the SQL types supported by Java. Also, there is no mention of any program variables in the *registerOutParameter( )* method. Values are pulled from the database to the program by using the familiar *getXXX( )* methods. However, this can only be done after the *CallableStatement* has been executed. Since the available procedure only queries the database, we can use the *executeQuery( )* method, for example,

```
hasTape.executeQuery();
```

Now we can pull the information from the procedure with the *getInt( )* method, such as

```
int tapeID = hasTape.getInt(2);
```

With IN/OUT parameters, all of the steps for both IN and OUT parameters must be followed. Specifically, this means we must

1. Use the appropriate *setXXX( )* method to pass in a value
2. Use *registerOutParameter( )* to set the appropriate SQL type
3. Use the appropriate *getXXX( )* method to retrieve the value after executing the query

Stored procedures can also return values. Such procedures are sometimes called *stored functions*. The syntax for accessing stored functions by a *CallableStatement* is

```
prepareCall("{? = call function_name(?, ? . . . ?)}");
```

The value returned by the stored function can be a simple value, or it can be a *ResultSet*, or even multiple *ResultSets* (in which case, the *execute( )* method must be used to perform the function call). For simple return values in stored functions, the placeholder is treated exactly the same as an OUT parameter. The *registerOutParameter( )* method is called with 1 as the placeholder value, and the appropriate *getXXX( )* method retrieves the value.

If the return value is one or more *ResultSets*, DBMS-specific routines are needed to access the information. For example, with Oracle databases, the SQL type for the *registerOutParameter( )* method is OracleTypes.Cursor. As a result, this topic is beyond the scope of this guide. The only fact we will mention is that all *ResultSets* should be accessed before any IN/OUT or OUT parameters are retrieved.

The program example demonstrating *CallableStatements* is CallableJDBC. This program accesses the stored procedure customer_has. In theory, using stored procedures should result in better performance. (See Section 3.4 for a test example.)

CallableJDBC

```
1   import java.sql.*;
2   import javax.swing.*;
3   import java.awt.event.*;
4   import java.util.*;
5
6   public class CallableJDBC extends JTableJDBC {
7       ConnectionJDBC CJ = null;
8       Connection dbConnect = null;
9       CallableStatement dbStatement = null;
10
11      public static void main(String args[]) {
12          CallableJDBC PJ = new CallableJDBC("CallableStatement Example");
13          PJ.show();
14          PJ.pack();
15      }
16
17      public CallableJDBC(String text) {
18          super(text);
19          inputLabel.setText("Tape ID Number");
20          try {
21              CJ = new ConnectionJDBC();
22              dbConnect = CJ.makeConnection("jdbc:oracle:oci8:@",
23                                            "jdbc_user","guest");
24              dbStatement = dbConnect.prepareCall("{call customer_has(?,?,?)}");
25          } catch (SQLException sqlex) {
26              JOptionPane.showMessageDialog(null,sqlex.getMessage());
27          }
28      }
29
30      public void actionPerformed(ActionEvent evt) {
31          int tapeId = Integer.parseInt(inputText.getText().trim());//in GUIJDBC
32          try {
33              dbStatement.setInt(1,tapeId);
34              dbStatement.registerOutParameter(2,Types.VARCHAR);
35              dbStatement.registerOutParameter(3,Types.VARCHAR);
36              dbStatement.executeQuery();
37              presentCallableStatement(dbStatement); //from JTableJDBC
38          } catch (SQLException sqlex) {
39              System.out.println(sqlex.getMessage());
40          }
41      }
```

```
42
43      public void presentCallableStatement(CallableStatement cs)
44          throws SQLException {
45          Vector dataVector = new Vector();
46          Vector rowVector = new Vector();
47          rowVector.addElement(cs.getString(2));
48          rowVector.addElement(cs.getString(3));
49          dataVector.addElement(rowVector);
50          Vector headVector = new Vector(2);
51          headVector.addElement("Customer");
52          headVector.addElement("Phone");
53          dataTable = new JTable(dataVector, headVector); //from JTableJDBC
54          dataTableScrollPane.setViewportView(dataTable); //from JTableJDBC
55      }
56
57      public void exitWindow(int i) {
58          CJ.closeConnection(dbConnect,dbStatement);
59          System.exit(i);
60      }
61  }
```

CallableJDBC

The data members for CallableJDBC are similar to PreparedJDBC, except that we have a *CallableStatement* object instead of a *PreparedStatement*. The main( ) method is simple and obvious.

In the constructor (lines 17–28), there are a couple of subtle differences. First, since the query is slightly different, the text for the input field is changed in line 19. Second, we use the Oracle JDBC driver to make the connection in lines 22 and 23. However, this connection parameter does not specify the name of the driver, just the URL, username, and password. In order for this program to execute correctly, the driver must be loaded when the program is executed by setting the "jdbc.drivers" property. For example, if the program is executed from the command line, the command would be

```
java -cp oracle.jar;. -Djdbc.drivers="oracle.jdbc.driver.OracleDriver" CallableJDBC
```

Line 24 contains the *prepareCall( )* method, with the call to the "customer_has" stored procedure.

CallableJDBC has to override the actionPerformed( ) method, since setting up a call to a stored procedure is different than executing a query in JDBC. The value of the tape ID is again retrieved from the inputText field and converted into an integer. The setInt( ) method in line 33 assigns this value to the input parameter of the stored procedure. As usual with JDBC objects, the parameters are numbered starting with 1. The two output parameters are registered in lines 34 and 35. In both cases, the values returned by the stored procedure are strings. However, we must use the SQL type, VARCHAR, to indicate the type being returned. Line 36 executes the query.

In all of the other examples, after the query is executed, a *ResultSet* is generated and some means of presenting the values in the *ResultSet* is employed. *CallableStatements* are fundamentally different, in that the output parameters of the stored procedure must be accessed from the *CallableStatement*, not a *ResultSet*. If a *ResultSet* is returned by a stored function, after it is retrieved, it is processed as normal. In line 37, we call a new method, presentCallableStatement( ), in order to display the values returned in the output parameters of the stored procedure.

The method presentCallableStatement is in lines 43-55. We are using the *Vector* of *Vector* approach to hold the information presented by a *JTable*. The dataVector contains only one row, so we do not need to loop over the possible values. Lines 47 and 48 retrieve the values from the output parameters and place them in the *Vector*. The headVector contains the strings for the titles. Note that, as in JTableJDBC, we create the headVector every time the user performs the query. Finally, in lines 53 and 54, the new *JTable* is created and is set to the view of the *JScrollPane*. The last method in the class closes the connection whenever the user exits the program. Lines 57-60 are called when the user closes the window.

3.3 **API Summary**

This chapter has covered the advanced mechanisms for querying the database. The primary interfaces and methods are

- *PreparedStatement*
  - *setXXX(String SQLQueryColumnName)*
  - *setXXX(int SQLQueryColumnNumber)*
  - *executeQuery( )*
- *CallableStatement*
  - *prepareCall(String storedProcedureCall)*
  - *registerOutParameter(int PlaceholderNumber, SQLType)*

3.4 **Going Beyond**

1. *PreparedStatements* can be used in all of the examples of Chapter 2. Rewrite the JDBC2TableModel.java and Serialized.java to use *PreparedStatements* instead of *Statements*.

2. Run tests to determine if your database benefits from *PreparedStatements*. Modify PreparedJDBC.java to include timing information and to execute a very long query many times (with different parameters). One possible example is to generate a list of customers who have never rented a given title. Then modify the program to use *Statements* instead of *PreparedStatements*. Determine which is faster.

3. If possible for your driver/database combination, modify CallableJDBC.java so that the stored procedure returns multiple *ResultSet* objects. Display the *ResultSets* as an array of *JTables*. Each *JTable* should be inside its own *JScrollPane*. Place all of the *JScrollPanes* inside a *JTabbedPane*. This is a complicated problem, but it provides tremendous amounts of well-organized information to the user.

4. Run tests to determine if your database benefits from stored procedures and *Callable-Statements*. Modify CallableJDBC.java to include timing information and to access a stored procedure of a very long query many times (with different parameters). One possible example is to generate a list of customers who have never rented a given title. Then modify the program to use *Statements* and *PreparedStatements* instead of *CallableStatements*. Determine which is faster.

5. An alternative to presenting information in *JTable* format is to create a *JLabel* and *JTextField* for each value. Given that *CallableStatements* without return values can only return one set of values, modify CallableJDBC so that it uses this format to present the results of the query.

chapter **4**

Updating the Database

In Chapters 2 and 3, different techniques are used for presenting information to the user and querying the database. Although queries dominate most database applications, it is a rare database environment that is static. As such, we need to modify the information in the database. Within SQL, the three commands to modify the database are Update, Insert, and Delete. There is little difference in how JDBC handles the three cases, so the examples here focus on the more common operations of Update and Insert. In this chapter, we discuss a simple update program to add tapes to an inventory one at a time; a sophisticated update mechanism that allows several updates to be processed at once; and the update mode for JDBC 2.0 *ResultSets* to have a customer return a tape.

4.1 Simple Updates

Performing basic update operations is almost identical to performing queries. The only two differences are that 1) the SQL command must be Update, Insert, or Delete, and 2) the *Statement* method *executeUpdate()* is used instead of *executeQuery()*. The program example UpdateJDBC.java is an update using this straightforward approach.

UpdateJDBC

```
1   import java.sql.*;
2   import javax.swing.*;
3   import java.awt.event.*;
4
5   public class UpdateJDBC extends GUIJDBC {
6       public UpdateJDBC() {
7           super("Adding Copies of Videos");
8           inputLabel.setText("Title ID Number");//from GUIJDBC
9           inputButton.setText("Insert");//from GUIJDBC
10      }
```

```
11
12      public static void main(String args[]) {
13          UpdateJDBC UJ = new UpdateJDBC();
14          UJ.show();
15          UJ.pack();
16      }
17
18      public void actionPerformed(ActionEvent evt) {
19          String update = "Insert into Tapes (Select max(TapeId)+1, " +
20              inputText.getText().trim() + ",'VHS' from Tapes)";
21          ConnectionJDBC CJ = new ConnectionJDBC();
22          Connection dbConnect = null;
23          Statement dbStatement = null;
24          try {
25              dbConnect =
26                  CJ.makeConnection("oracle.jdbc.driver.OracleDriver",
27                              "jdbc:oracle:oci8:@","jdbc_user","guest");
28              dbStatement = dbConnect.createStatement();
29              int updateCount = dbStatement.executeUpdate(update);
30              JOptionPane.showMessageDialog(null,updateCount + " tape added");
31          } catch (SQLException sqlex) {
32              JOptionPane.showMessageDialog(null,sqlex.getMessage());
33          }
34          finally {
35              CJ.closeConnection(dbConnect,dbStatement);
36          }
37      }
38  }
```

UpdateJDBC

UpdateJDBC extends the GUIJDBC program in order to use a GUI. The user enters the ID of the Title, then the program inserts a new copy of the tape into the database. In lines 8 and 9, the labels for inputLabel and inputButton are changed to represent the new application.

The only other change to GUIJDBC is the actionPerformed() method. First, we create an SQL Insert statement in lines 19 and 20. The parameter value from the user is "inputText.getText().trim()" in line 20. The other values are a new maximum TapeId and a literal of 'VHS' for the tape type. The rest of the actionPerformed method should be very familiar by now. We create a ConnectionJDBC object in line 21, then declare a *Connection* object and a *Statement* object in the next two lines. Within a try block, we make a connection (using the parameters for a local version of an Oracle database) and create a statement. In line 28, we execute the update by using the *executeUpdate()* method of the *Statement* interface. If there is an error, we display it to the user. At the end, we close the connection to the database.

4.2   Batch Updates

PreparedStatements can also be used to update the database. The *PreparedStatement* object is created in exactly the same way as in Section 3.1, only the SQL statement is an Insert, Update, or Delete statement. For example, to create a PreparedStatement to insert a row into the Customer table,

```
PreparedStatement pStmt = dbConnect.prepareStatement(
                          "Insert into customers values ( ?, ?, ?, ?)");
```

Just as with a query, we use the setXXX( ) methods to fill in the values for the placeholders. Sometimes when inserting a row into a table, not all of the values will be known. Thus, we want to insert a null value into the database. One of the methods in the PreparedStatement interface is *setNull( )*. The *setNull( )* method takes two parameters: the placeholder location in the query string, and an SQL type. The valid SQL types are found in the class *Types* in the java.sql package. For example, if we did not know a customer's address, but had all of the other information in appropriately named strings, we could use the following set of method calls to fill the *PreparedStatement* object pStmt:

```
pStmt.setInt(1,CustId);
pStmt.setString(2, CustName);
pStmt.setNull(3, Types.VARCHAR);
pStmt.setString(4, CustPhone);
```

Under JDBC 2.0, there is an optional method we can use to speed up the processing of a large number of similar database updates. Although the API states that this method can be used with *Statement* objects, it is most commonly supported with *PreparedStatements*. Under this mechanism, we can request the database to perform all of the updates at one time. This is called a *batch update*. In order to perform batch updates, we have to do two things. First, we have to create a batch, then we have to call the *executeBatch( )* method.

Creating a batch is accomplished by adding each *PreparedStatement* to the batch. After every placeholder has been set, the method *addBatch( )* is called. All of the placeholder values are added to a group that will be sent to the database together.

```
pStmt.addBatch();
```

When the *executeBatch( )* method is called, all of the updates are applied to the database. The method returns an array of integers. There is one element in the array for each *PreparedStatement* added to the batch. The value of each element is the number of rows updated by the corresponding *PreparedStatement*. In our example with inserting values, the logical value for each element in the array would be 1, but some driver/database combinations cannot determine the number of rows modified by arbitrary SQL Insert statements. If the *PreparedStatement* is pStmt, a batch of updates could be executed with

```
int[] ups = pStmt.executeBatch();
```

If any of the updates fail, the *executeBatch( )* method throws a special subclass of *SQLException* called *BatchUpdateException*. In addition to the information in *SQLExceptions*,

BatchUpdateExceptions also contain all of the update counts that successfully completed
before the exception. These counts can be retrieved by calling the method *getUpdateCounts( )*.
Unfortunately, the Java 2 Standard Edition version 1.3 still defines the *executeBatch( )* method
to throw an *SQLException*. This means we have to do some typecasting to find the problem. As
an example,

```
int[] ups=((BatchUpdateException)sqlex).getUpdateCounts();
```

will provide each integer in the integer array "ups" with the number of successful update values
before the exception.

Although batch updates are quite powerful, they do come with some drawbacks. If there is
an exception, it is not discovered until the *executeBatch( )* method call. Suppose we are inserting
400 rows into a table. If the second row has an error, we will still process all 400 rows before we
discover the problem. Secondly, the *executeBatch( )* method is optional, which means that not
all driver/database combinations support it. Even using those driver/database combinations
that do support it, the execution of the method may not be as expected. For example, using
an Oracle database and the Oracle OCI8 driver, a successful *PreparedStatement* batch update
returns a value of −2 for each *PreparedStatement* in the batch. The value of −2 indicates that
the operation is successful, but the true number of updated rows is unknown. Also note that
the placeholders set in a setXXX( ) method are not preserved across calls to *addBatch( )*. We
must set all of the placeholders for each call.

The program example demonstrating batch updates is BatchUpdateJDBC.java. This program is similar to the simple update program in Section 4.1, except it inserts a random number
(5–9) of tapes into the database.

BatchUpdateJDBC

```
1   import java.sql.*;
2   import javax.swing.*;
3   import java.awt.event.*;
4
5   public class BatchUpdateJDBC extends GUIJDBC {
6       public BatchUpdateJDBC() {
7           super("Batch Updates to Add Copies");
8           inputLabel.setText("Title ID Number");
9           inputButton.setText("Insert");
10      }
11
12      public static void main(String args[]) {
13          BatchUpdateJDBC BUJ = new BatchUpdateJDBC();
14          BUJ.show();
15          BUJ.pack();
16      }
17
18      public void actionPerformed(ActionEvent evt) {
```

```
19    String update = "Insert into Tapes ( " +
20        "Select max(TapeId)+1, ?, 'VHS' from Tapes)";
21    ConnectionJDBC CJ = new ConnectionJDBC();
22    Connection dbConnect = null;
23    PreparedStatement dbStatement = null;
24    try {
25        dbConnect =
26            CJ.makeConnection("oracle.jdbc.driver.OracleDriver",
27                            "jdbc:oracle:oci8:@","jdbc_user","guest");
28        dbStatement = dbConnect.prepareStatement(update);
29        int tapeCount = (int)(Math.random()*5) +5;
30        for (int i=0; i<tapeCount; i++) {
31            dbStatement.
32                setInt(1, Integer.parseInt(inputText.getText().trim()));
33            dbStatement.addBatch();
34        }
35        dbStatement.executeBatch();
36        JOptionPane.showMessageDialog(null,"Insert successful");
37    } catch (SQLException sqlex) {
38        JOptionPane.showMessageDialog(null,sqlex.getMessage());
39    }
40    finally {
41        CJ.closeConnection(dbConnect,dbStatement);
42    }
43 }
44 }
```

BatchUpdateJDBC

The significant differences between UpdateJDBC and BatchUpdateJDBC appear in the actionPerformed( ) method, which occupies almost the entire BatchUpdateJDBC class. The first difference is in the update string in lines 19-20. In BatchUpdateJDBC, we want to use *PreparedStatments*, so we use the placeholder "?" to indicate the location for the value entered by the user. Line 23 is another difference, as we declare a *PreparedStatement* object instead of a *Statement* object. In line 28, we use the *prepareStatement( )* method, passing in the update query. We use a random-number generator to determine the number of tapes to be added for this title in line 29. Lines 30-34 form a loop to create the batch for the update. In each case, we input the value from the GUI into the *PreparedStatement* (line 32), then add that update to the batch (line 33). Line 35 executes all of the updates created in the loop. The updates are executed one at a time, and each is committed before the next starts. This allows the TapeId to be incremented for each update. Appropriate messages are displayed to the user in case of success (line 36) or failure (line 38). In any event, the connection is closed once the update is finished.

4.3   Updating through *ResultSets*

In Section 2.3, we use the dynamic access methods of the *ResultSet* interface. The *create-Statement( )* method accepts another parameter indicating the concurrency capability of the generated *ResultSet*. There are two types of concurrency possible:

1. CONCUR_READ_ONLY: This *resultSetConcurrency* is the default. The database cannot be updated through the *ResultSet*.

2. CONCUR_UPDATABLE: This *resultSetConcurrency* allows changes to the database through the *ResultSet*. However, an update can be processed through a *ResultSet* only if the query meets the following three conditions: it references only one table; does not contain a JOIN or GROUP BY clause; and selects the primary key of the table. Furthermore, if an insert is attempted, any column not selected by the query must have a default value or accept null as a value.

There are three steps required to update the database through a *ResultSet:* First, the cursor has to be placed on the correct row. Second, the field must be updated to the desired value with the appropriate *updateXXX( )* method. Third, the method *updateRow( )* is called to send the update to the database.

The *updateXXX( )* methods work like a cross between the *getXXX( ) ResultSet* methods and the *PreparedStatement* setXXX( ) methods. They accept two parameters. The first is the column number or name (as in *getXXX( )* parameters) and the second is the value (as in setXXX( ) parameters). As with the setXXX( ) methods, the type of the method must be compatible with the database type of the column. For example, if the query is "Select Order_Number, Status from Orders where CustomerID=999" and we wanted to update the Orders table to set the status to 'I' for a tape rented to CustomerID 999,

```
rs.absolute(1);
rs.updateString(2,'I');
rs.updateRow();
```

would update the Orders table. An example of how to insert a row through a *ResultSet* is in Section 5.3.

The program example to demonstrate updating the database through a query returned to the user is UpdateResultSetJDBC.java. It uses an *AbstractTableModel* class, UpdateTableModel, to present the information. In this example, the user enters a customer Id and sees the familiar list of all tapes checked out by the customer. By selecting a tape and clicking the "Return" button, the database is updated to indicate that the tape is returned. As usual in cases with a *TableModel* class, we present UpdateTableModel first.

UpdateTableModel

```
1   import java.sql.*;
2
3   public class UpdateTableModel extends JDBC2TableModel {
```

```
4
5        public UpdateTableModel() {
6            super();
7            try {
8                dbStatement = dbConnect.  //from JDBC2TableModel
9                    createStatement(ResultSet.TYPE_SCROLL_SENSITIVE,
10                                    ResultSet.CONCUR_UPDATABLE);
11           } catch (SQLException sqlex) {
12               System.out.println(sqlex.getMessage());
13           }
14       }
15
16       public void update(int row) {
17           try {
18               dbRS.absolute(row+1); //from JDBC2TableModel
19               dbRS.updateString(5,"I");
20               dbRS.updateRow();
21           } catch (SQLException sqlex) {
22               System.out.println(sqlex.getMessage());
23           }
24       }
25   }
```

UpdateTableModel

UpdateTableModel extends JDBC2TableModel, so that many of the methods defined there can be used (such as getRow(), getCount(), and getValueAt()). The only changes are to the constructor and the new method, update(). Within the constructor, we change the parameters to the *createStatement()* method, setting the *resultSetConcurrency* parameter to ResultSet.CONCUR_UPDATABLE in line 10. This allows the Java program to update the database after looking at the values in the *ResultSet*.

The update() method in lines 16–24 performs the update to the database. The parameter to the update method is the *JTable* row that the user has selected to update. As usual, JDBC API methods start numbering with 1, while swing API methods start numbering at 0, so we have to add 1 to the *JTable* row to determine the corresponding *ResultSet* row. In line 18, we use the *absolute()* method to move the cursor to the correct row. The *updateString()* method changes the value of the fifth field in the current row in the *ResultSet* to the string "I". Line 20 is the command to submit the update to the database, via the *updateRow()* method. As usual, if there is a problem, we display an error message, but note that UpdateTableModel displays the error message on the console instead of the user screen. It is left as an exercise for the reader to make the communication return all the way to the user.

UpdateResultSetJDBC

```
1   import java.util.*;
2   import java.awt.event.*;
3   import javax.swing.*;
4
5   public class UpdateResultSetJDBC extends TableModelJDBC2 {
6       UpdateTableModel utm = null;
7
8       public static void main(String args[]) {
9           UpdateResultSetJDBC upRS = new
10              UpdateResultSetJDBC("Return Video Screen");
11          upRS.show();
12          upRS.pack();
13      }
14
15      public UpdateResultSetJDBC(String title) {
16          super(title);
17          inputButton.setText("Return"); // from GUIJDBC
18          utm = new UpdateTableModel();
19          Vector headVector = new Vector(4);
20          headVector.addElement("Order Number");
21          headVector.addElement("Customer ID");
22          headVector.addElement("Tape ID");
23          headVector.addElement("Due Date");
24          utm.setHeading(headVector); // from JDBCTableModel
25          dataTable.setSelectionMode
26              (ListSelectionModel.SINGLE_SELECTION); // from JTableJDBC
27          dataTable.setModel(utm); // from JTableJDBC
28      }
29
30      public void actionPerformed(ActionEvent evt) {
31          if (evt.getSource() == inputButton) { //from GUIJDBC
32              int item = dataTable.getSelectedRow(); //from JTableJDBC
33              if (item!=-1) {
34                  utm.update(item);
35                  dataTable.clearSelection(); //from JTableJDBC
36              }
37          }
38          getResultSet();
39      }
40
41      public void getResultSet() {
42          String query = "Select OrderNumber, CustomerID, TapeID, " +
43              "DueDate, Status " +
44              "From Orders " +
45              "Where Status ='0' and " +
```

```
46                "CustomerID= " + inputText.getText().trim(); //from GUIJDBC
47          utm.showQuery(query); // from JDBC2TableModel
48          dataTableScrollPane.setViewportView(dataTable); //from JTableJDBC
49       }
50
51       public void exitWindow(int i) {
52          utm.closeConnection();
53          System.exit(i);
54       }
55   }
```

UpdateResultSetJDBC

The GUI part of the program is straightforward. We first declare an UpdateTableModel object that we can use to access the database. The main method creates the UpdateResult-SetJDBC object and displays it on the screen. The constructor method in lines 15–28 creates the user interface components by modifying the inherited elements. The text on inputButton is changed to "Return" to indicate that the user is returning the tape. The headings for the *JTable* are set by loading a *Vector* with four strings, and then calling the method setHeading( ). We modify the *SelectionMode* of dataTable so that only one row can be selected at a time in lines 25 and 26.

When the user clicks the "Return" button, the actionPerformed( ) method is called. In this example, we want to do different things for clicking the button and hitting Enter in the inputText field. When the user hits Enter, the tapes checked out to the user should be returned, but when the "Return" button is clicked, an update should be performed. (Note that if no tape is selected and the "Return" button is pressed, the result is the same as hitting Enter in the *JTextField*.) This is a feature. In line 31, we check the source of the event, and if it is the inputButton, we try to update the database. First, we use the *getSelectedRow( )* method of the *JTable* class. This method will return the count of the highlighted row, or –1 if no row is selected. If a row is selected, the row number is passed to the update( ) method of the UpdateTableModel object. After the update, the selection is cleared in line 35.

In any event, the last step of actionPerformed( ) is to get a new *ResultSet* to be displayed, by calling the getResultSet( ) method of lines 41–49. Note that the query called in getResultSet( ) returns all five attributes of the Orders table, but lists them specifically, as opposed to the Select * style. This is required by the database/driver combination in order to update the database through the *ResultSet*. Also note that since only four fields are placed in the heading *Vector* (lines 19–24), only the first four fields are displayed to the user. See Figure 4.1 for a screen shot of the user interface. The query string is then passed to the method showQuery( ), defined in JDBC2TableModel.java. In line 48, we display the resulting dataTable in the *JScrollPane*. Finally, in lines 51–54, the interface signals the table model when it is time to close the connection (e.g., when the user closes the window).

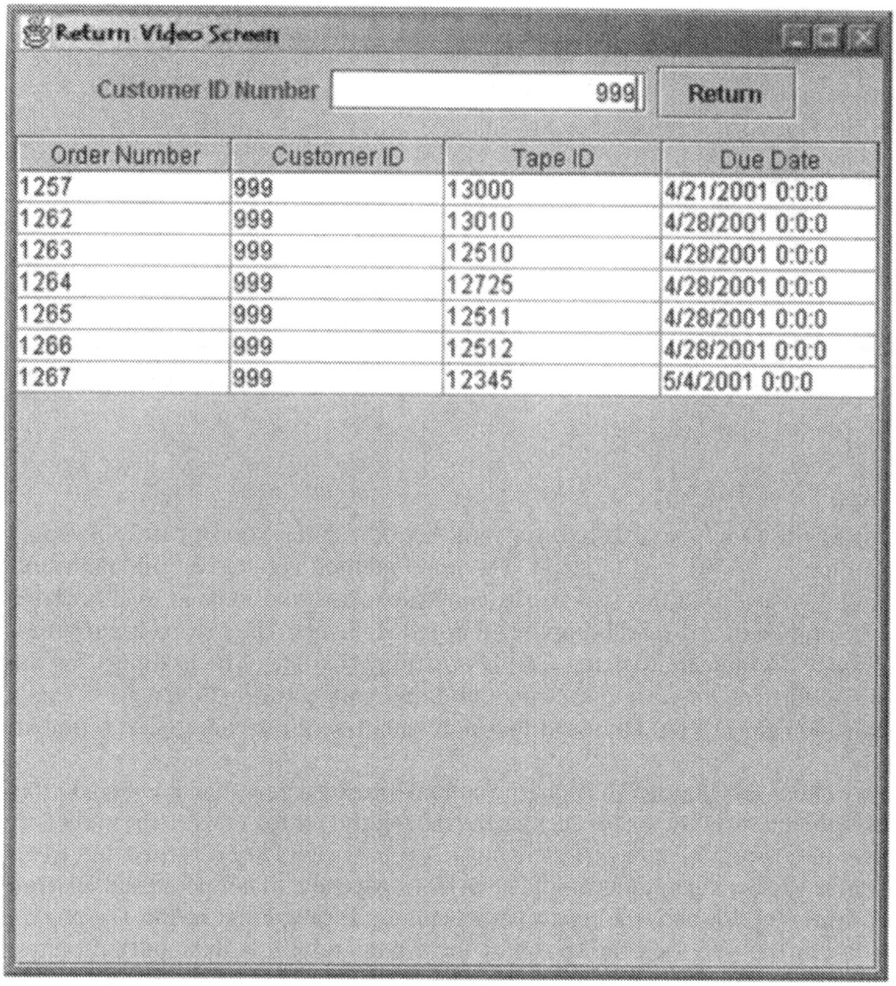

Figure 4.1: Updating through *ResultSets*.

4.4 API Summary

In this chapter, various ways to update the database have been discussed. There are three primary mechanisms. The interfaces and methods required for updating the database are

- *Statement*
    - *executeUpdate(String SQLUpdateString)*
- *PreparedStatement*
    - *addBatch( )*
    - *executeBatch( )*

- *Connection*
  - *createStatement(ResultSetType ScrollingANDSensitivity, ResultSetConcurrency ReadOnlyORUpdatable)*
- *ResultSet*
  - *updateXXX(int PlaceholderNumber, Object Value)*
  - *updateRow( )*

4.5 Going Beyond

1. Batch updates are supposed to make large numbers of insertions quicker. See if your system performs as expected. Modify BatchUpdateJDBC.java so that it includes timing information. Increase the number of inserts to a large enough number that a noticeable amount of time is required to perform the update. Perform the same update using simple updates, as in UpdateJDBC.java. Determine which is faster.

2. Modify UpdateJDBC so that it does not create a new connection for every update request.

3. Create a program to update the customer information. Allow the user to enter a customer ID. Show the results to the user (there should be one row returned by the database) in a format where each field in the table is its own *JTextField* with its own *JLabel*. Allow the user to update any or all of the fields, then update the database. Use both simple updates and updating through *ResultSets*. Which approach is more natural?

chapter **5**

Advanced JDBC Topics

Now that the basics of JDBC have been covered, I'll move on to advanced parts of the system. These topics require greater understanding of databases and Java than those in the previous chapters. However, mastering them will provide benefits in many programming applications. The four topics covered here are JDBC drivers, metadata, binary large objects (as an example of SQL3 data types), and transactions. For the last three, there is a program example to demonstrate each concept.

5.1 Drivers

In our examples, we use three different drivers. In all three cases, we need a driver name and a URL to find the database. In some cases, we need a username and a password as well. Table 5.1 lays out the information for each driver.

The *DriverManager* class must select the appropriate *driver* from the ones already loaded. In each of the examples, either the driver is passed to the makeConnection( ) method in ConnectionJDBC, or a default (the ODBC column in the table) is used. In each case, the class must be in a file in the classpath of the JVM in order for it to be loaded. The first class is included in Java 2 Standard Edition, Version 1.3. The second driver can be downloaded from the web site, in the file *oracle.jar*. The third driver is also available on the web site in the file *postgresql.jar*. The fact that these classes all end in "Driver" is meaningless, as the drivers could be called anything. The "." notation is used to indicate the path within the jar file to find the class. This is helpful if the source code is available, such as with the PostgreSQL driver, in order to examine the actual code used to build drivers. For example, if the PostgreSQL source tree for the driver is the directory /home, the Driver java file would be /home/org/postgresql/Driver.java.

Another parameter required to make a connection to the database is called "URL" in the table. It defines the protocol for the *Driver*. All three drivers use "jdbc:" as the protocol. This is similar to how URLs on web pages start with "http:" to indicate that they are using the hypertext transfer protocol. All URLs for JDBC drivers should start with "jdbc."

Table 5.1: JDBC Driver Comparison

Database	ODBC	Oracle	PostgreSQL
Jar File	None	oracle.jar	postgres.jar
Driver Type	1	4	4
Driver	sun.jdbc.odbc .JdbcOdbcDriver	oracle.jdbc.driver .OracleDriver	org.postgresql.Driver
URL	jdbc:odbc:jdbc_ book	jdbc:oracle:oci8:@	jdbc:postgresql:host/jdbc_book
Username	None	jdbc_user	jdbc_user
Password	None	guest	guest

The next part of the URL starts the subprotocol. There are no restrictions on the contents of the subprotocol, so it is product-specific. In each of the three drivers, the subprotocol tells us something about the driver itself. The bridge has "odbc:," indicating that the driver is a JDBC–ODBC bridge, or Type 1 driver. The Oracle driver has "oracle" as the subprotocol, while the PostgreSQL driver has "postgresql."

The third part of the Oracle subprotocol is different from the other two. It consists of "oci8:." Oracle has two different drivers currently in use. (A third, older driver (OCI7) is still supported, but Oracle encourages users to move to the newer versions.) The one we are using here is the OCI8 driver, while the other is the "thin" driver. The protocol for the thin driver starts (not surprisingly) with "jdbc:oracle:thin:." The OCI8 driver is designed for applications, while the thin driver is designed for applets. Since our Oracle examples are based on applications, we use the OCI8 driver.

The next part of each driver is the location of the database. With the bridge, the database must be an ODBC data source on the local machine. Therefore, the name is simply the data source name, "jdbc_book." In the Oracle case, the "@" is usually followed by the machine name hosting the database. However, there is also a default database available on each machine. In our case, we are using the default database, so we don't have to list anything after the "@." The PostgreSQL driver needs a full IP address of the machine running the database. If the database is on the same machine as the JDBC program, "localhost" can be used as the machine name.

In both the Oracle and PostgreSQL drivers, a port number can follow the machine name. In both cases, we use the default port—1521—so no port numbers are needed. Finally, the database name is given to the Oracle and PostgreSQL drivers. The name of the database for all of our examples is "jdbc_book."

In order to modify the program examples to use a different driver, the driver name, URL, and (if needed) username and password must be passed to the makeConnection() method of ConnectionJDBC. All of this information should be available in the documentation for the driver. The jar file containing the driver must also be in a directory accessible by the JVM.

Now that we've seen some more details about our driver examples, we need to look at drivers in general. In the analogy in Section 1.1, a driver is compared to a bridge over a river.

Just as there are different types of bridges (girder, suspension, etc.), there are different types of drivers. Unfortunately, unlike bridges, the types of drivers have rather boring names—Type 1, Type 2, Type 3, and Type 4. The Sun web site has a listing of available drivers (the guide's web site links to the page).

Type 1 Drivers.   The default driver in ConnectionJDBC is an example of a Type 1 driver. This driver is called a "bridge" because it provides JDBC via an ODBC driver. On the web site, there are instructions to set up the Microsoft Access database as an ODBC data source in order to use the JDBC examples. Clearly, such drivers are limited in terms of their effectiveness over the Internet, but for certain in-house applications using existing ODBC data, Type 1 drivers can work well. As of June 2001, there are only ten Type 1 drivers in the Sun online listing. As to the driver we are using in our examples, the Sun web site states, "The JDBC-ODBC bridge driver is recommended only for experimental use or when no other alternative is available."

Type 2 Drivers.   Type 2 drivers convert JDBC API calls, such as *createStatement( )*, into calls to a specific database API. In order for these calls to be executed, there must exist software on the client machine that implements them. All of the network communication is done via the specific database software. In our analogy, the corresponding bridge would only allow blue cars made in 1998 to cross to the factory. If we've got a 1998 blue car, that's great, but we probably don't want to go buy one just to use this bridge. As a result, Type 2 drivers are not appropriate for Internet applications, but they work well in environments where the client software is commonly installed, such as within a company. There are 24 Type 2 drivers in the online listing.

Type 3 and Type 4 Drivers.   Both Type 3 and Type 4 drivers are implemented entirely in Java and don't require any special client software, beyond the Java code for the driver, to execute. This makes them popular choices for Internet applications. There are 54 Type 3 drivers listed in the online catalog, and 87 Type 4 drivers. The difference between them is how the connection is made to the server. Type 3 drivers use a DBMS-independent protocol, while Type 4 drivers use a DBMS-specific protocol to access the database. Type 3 drivers make it easier to transfer applications from one database to another. In our analogy, the bridge representing a Type 3 driver could have roads going to totally different factories, say, to a chair factory and a table factory. On the other hand, while a bridge representing a Type 4 driver could lead to many chair factories, it could not be used to get to a table factory. As a tradeoff, sometimes Type 4 drivers can take advantage of specific features within a DBMS that are not available on other systems. This means Type 4 drivers have better performance than Type 3 drivers for some applications.

   In this guide, we are using Type 4 drivers for the Oracle and PostgreSQL databases, but the choice between Type 3 and Type 4 should be based on project needs. Section 5.4 introduces one of the differences between various Type 4 drivers, specifically how the drivers treat binary large objects (BLOBs).

5.2 Metadata

Databases allow users to define tables, keys, domains, columns, and more. The only way a database can manage data without knowing the schema in advance is to have metadata—that is, data about the data. The metadata describes the data in a consistent format. This allows the database to manage data through the description rather than through the actual data.

Metadata can also be used within JDBC to help manage data. Using metadata can help with access and presentation of data, as well as allow independence between the program and the database. There are two types of metadata available in JDBC: the *DatabaseMetaData* interface and the *ResultSetMetaData* interface.

The **DatabaseMetaData** *Interface.* The *DatabaseMetaData* interface provides information about the database as a whole. There are many methods within the interface, such as whether or not transactions are supported (see Section 5.3 for more on transactions) or whether or not JDBC 2.0-type result sets are supported (see Sections 2.3 and 4.3 for more on JDBC 2.0 ResultSets). These methods are very important for making a JDBC program as portable as possible, since the use of advanced features is not supported in all driver/database combinations. Usually, if a feature is not supported, testing for the support will generate an *SQLException*. The *DatabaseMetaData* interface also provides a means to find out about the schema. There is a method to retrieve the names of the tables available, as well as the name of the stored procedures available (see Section 3.2 for more on stored procedures). There are methods to return primary keys, foreign keys, and user-defined types.

The **ResultSetMetaData** *Interface.* While the *DatabaseMetaData* interface applies to the entire database, the *ResultSetMetaData* interface applies to one particular result set generated by one particular query. The *ResultSetMetaData* interface has far fewer methods, only 21 in Java 2 Standard Edition version 1.3. However, these methods allow a great deal of flexibility in terms of performing queries against a database, especially if the entire query is not known a priori. For a particular query, the *ResultSetMetaData* interface methods can tell us the number of columns with *getColumnCount( )*, the name of each column with *getColumnName(column)*, the display size of each column with *getColumnDisplaySize(column)*, and the SQL type of each column with *getColumnType(column)*.

For example, in order to generate query-independent headings for a *JTable* (see Section 2.1 for details), given a *ResultSetMetaData* object rsmd, we could use the loop

```
for (int i=1; i<=rsmd.getColumnCount(); i++)
  { headVector.addElement(rsmd.getColumnName(i)); }
```

Again, columns are numbered starting from 1, while the typical Java structure numbers start from 0. Also notice that the *ResultSetMetaData* methods require the integer position and cannot take a string with the name of the query object.

The program example using the *ResultSetMetaData* interface is MetaDataJDBC.java. This program accepts an arbitrary SQL query and outputs the results by placing each field on its own line. This means that a query returning 25 rows each with 4 fields would generate 100 lines of output. This program is relatively fragile and under some circumstances will generate unexpected output. The problem centers around the type of data in the field. Although it is possible to do type checking (using more *ResultSetMetaData* methods), a comprehensive example is beyond the scope of this guide.

MetaDataJDBC

```
1   import java.sql.*;
2
3   public class MetaDataJDBC extends ConnectionJDBC {
4       public static void main(String args[]) {
5           if (args.length != 1) {
6               System.out.println("Usage: java MetaDataJDBC SQLquery");
7               System.exit(1);
8           }
9
10          MetaDataJDBC MDJ = new MetaDataJDBC();
11          Connection dbConnect = null;
12          Statement dbStatement = null;
13          ResultSet dbRS = null;
14          try {
15              dbConnect = MDJ.makeConnection(); // from ConnectionJDBC
16              dbStatement = dbConnect.createStatement();
17              dbRS = dbStatement.executeQuery(args[0]);
18              MDJ.presentResultSet(dbRS);
19          } catch (SQLException sqlex) {
20              System.out.println(sqlex.getMessage());
21          }
22          finally {
23              MDJ.closeConnection(dbConnect,dbStatement); // from ConnectionJDBC
24          }
25      }
26
27      public void presentResultSet(ResultSet rs)
28          throws SQLException {
29          if (!rs.next()) System.out.println("No records found");
30          else {
31              ResultSetMetaData rsmd = rs.getMetaData();
32              do {
33                  for (int i=1; i<=rsmd.getColumnCount(); i++) {
34                      System.out.println(rsmd.getColumnLabel(i) + ":"
35                                          + rs.getObject(i));
36                  }
37              }while (rs.next());
38          }
39      }
40  }
```

MetaDataJDBC

MetaDataJDBC extends only the basic ConnectionJDBC program to take advantage of routines to connect to the database. In order to use the program, an SQL query must be entered as a single parameter, such as

```
java MetaDataJDBC "Select * from Customers"
```

from the command line under Windows systems. The main() method follows the common pattern of creating a ConnectionJDBC object (via a MetaDataJDBC object), making a connection to the database and creating a *Statement* object in lines 10-16. The entire query is sent to the *executeQuery()* method in line 17, and the familiar presentResultSet() method is called to display the results. Again, if there is a problem, we display an error message, and we always close the connection when the program is finished.

The presentResultSet() method in lines 27-39 is slightly different from the others. In this case, we do not know the names of the fields, or even how many fields are in each record. Line 29 checks to make sure that there is at least one row in the *ResultSet*. If there is at least one row, we use the *ResultSetMetaData* interface to provide the names of the fields for us. Line 31 creates the *ResultSetMetaData* object by using the *getMetaData()* method. The nested loop in lines 32-37 reads all of the rows in the *ResultSet* and for each row executes the inner loop. Line 33 uses the *getColumnCount()* method to determine the number of columns in the row. For each column, we output one line containing three fields. The first field is the name of the field as determined by the query. This means that the user can control the headings by using the SQL AS keyword within the Select clause. The second field is a simple separator. The third field is the value of the field. Since we do not know the type of the field, we use the *getObject()* method to retrieve the value. Since we are only outputting the value to the screen here, and all objects support the *toString()* method, this mechanism works, but sometimes the results are surprising.

5.3   Transactions

Under the default execution of the JDBC API, whenever a *Statement* object (or one of its subclasses) invokes the *executeQuery()*, *executeUpdate()*, or *execute()* methods, a transaction is started at the database. If the statement executes normally, the transaction commits. If an exception is thrown, the transaction aborts.

This behavior works very well so long as the SQL commands issued to the database are independent. However, this behavior can lead to unpredictable results if two (or more) SQL commands are related to each other. For example, suppose eVid allows customers to recheck a tape. This can be accomplished by first updating the current record to show that the tape is checked back in, and then inserting a new record with the new due date. However, if only the first update is successful, then the database will say that nobody has the tape—but it won't be in the store.

In order to allow a transaction to span multiple SQL commands, the *Connection* interface has the method *setAutoCommit()*. It accepts a Boolean parameter. If the Boolean passed to the method is *true*, then the default behavior is in force. If the Boolean value passed to the method is *false*, then the program must indicate to the database whether or not a transaction should commit. Not surprisingly, the *Connection* interface has the methods *commit()* and *rollback()*, which are called as needed. For example, if every part of a batch update (see Section 4.2) is successful, we would commit, whereas if the update throws an exception, we would roll back the transaction and perform none of the updates. This would prevent partial execution of batch updates. The code segment to do that is

```
try {
    try {
        pStmt.executeBatch();
        dbConnect.commit();
    } catch (SQLException sqlex) {
        dbConnect.rollback();
    }
} catch (SQLException sqlex) {} // catches the rollback exception
```

We have to use two nested try statements due to the fact that the *rollback( )* and *commit( )* methods both throw *SQLExceptions* if there is a problem. Unfortunately, if either of these methods fail, there is not much we can do, except possibly try them again. In either case, we would want the updates to be aborted, since a problem has occurred. Fortunately, there is nothing we need to do about the failure of the rollback statement, except close the connections. Eventually, the database will abort the transaction if it has not already done so.

In databases, transactions can operate at different levels of isolation. JDBC provides five levels of transaction isolation, and they are labeled by values in the *Connection* class. These isolation levels are

1. TRANSACTION_NONE: Transactions are not supported by the driver/database.

2. TRANSACTION_READ_UNCOMMITTED: Transactions are allowed to read uncommitted, or "dirty," values. These values are not guaranteed to be permanent in the database. If the transaction that produced the dirty values performs a rollback, then all transactions that read the dirty value must also roll back.

3. TRANSACTION_READ_COMMITTED: Transactions are only allowed to read committed values. However, another transaction may update rows in the *ResultSet* during the execution of our transaction. This can cause the values in the *ResultSet* to change if the query is repeated.

4. TRANSACTION_REPEATABLE_READ: Transactions are only allowed to read committed values, and no other transaction may update any of the rows in the *ResultSet*.

5. TRANSACTION_SERIALIZABLE: Transactions execute as if they are the only ones accessing the database. This prohibits any effect of any transaction from being visible, such as a transaction inserting a row into the database which satisfies a query.

We can check the isolation level with the *Connection* method *getTransactionIsolation( )*, and we can set it with the method *setTransactionIsolation( )*. For example, if dbConnect is the name of our *Connection* instance,

```
int isolation = dbConnect.getTransactionIsolation();
```

returns the transaction isolation level, while

```
dbConnect.setTransactionIsolation(TRANSACTION_SERIALIZABLE);
```

would set the isolation level to the highest value.

Unfortunately, every driver/database combination does not support every level of transaction isolation. For instance, Microsoft Access 97 under Windows 98 using the Sun JDBC-ODBC bridge driver will throw an exception if the *setTransactionIsolation( )* method is used. On the other hand, PostgreSQL 7.0.2 will not throw an exception, but it won't change the isolation level either. Under Oracle with the OCI8 driver, the only allowed isolation levels are TRANSACTION_READ_COMMITTED and TRANSACTION_SERIALIZABLE.

If different transaction levels are supported, the impact on performance must be considered. The higher the level of isolation, the more conflicts will be generated at the database. This will cause the overall database performance to degrade. It is very important to balance the needs of the application against this performance hit. In our other examples, we did not need any transaction control, so our programs ran as fast as possible. The program example to use transactions allows a customer to recheck a tape. It also shows how to insert new rows through a *ResultSet*. As with our other GUI programs, it uses a *TableModel*, and we present that first.

TransactionTableModel

```
1   import java.sql.*;
2
3   public class TransactionTableModel extends UpdateTableModel {
4       static final long MSECDAY = 86400000L;
5
6       public TransactionTableModel(){
7           super();
8           try {
9               dbConnect.setTransactionIsolation
10                  (Connection.TRANSACTION_SERIALIZABLE);
11          } catch (SQLException sqlex) {System.out.println(sqlex.getMessage());}
12      }
13
14      public void recheck(int row) {
15          try {
16              // dbConnect, dbStatement, and dbRS from JDBC2TableModel
17              dbConnect.setAutoCommit(false);
18              // This Statement finds the next order number
19              Statement stmt = dbConnect.createStatement();//from JDBC2TableModel
20              ResultSet rs = stmt.executeQuery("Select max(OrderNumber)+1 " +
21                                              "From Orders");
22              if (!rs.next()) {
23                  System.out.println("No tapes to return");
24                  return;
25              }
26              int newOrderNumber = rs.getInt(1);
```

```
27      int newCustomerID = Integer.parseInt
28          ((String)getValueAt(row,1)); //from JDBC2TableModel
29      int newTapeID = Integer.parseInt
30          ((String)getValueAt(row,2)); //from JDBC2TableModel
31      java.util.Date today = new java.util.Date();
32      java.sql.Date newDueDate =
33          new java.sql.Date(today.getTime()+5*MSECDAY);
34      dbRS.moveToInsertRow(); //from JDBC2TableModel
35      dbRS.updateInt(1,newOrderNumber);
36      dbRS.updateInt(2,newCustomerID);
37      dbRS.updateInt(3,newTapeID);
38      dbRS.updateDate(4,newDueDate);
39      dbRS.updateString(5,"0");
40      dbRS.insertRow();
41      dbRS.first();
42      update(row); //from UpdateTableModel
43      dbConnect.commit();
44      dbConnect.setAutoCommit(true);
45  } catch (SQLException sqlex) {
46      try {
47          dbConnect.rollback();
48          dbConnect.setAutoCommit(true);
49      } catch (SQLException sqlex2) {}
50  }
51  }
52 }
```

TransactionTableModel

Whenever a customer checks out a tape, we allow them five days to return it. In order to know when the five days are up, we need to know the number of milliseconds in a day (Java has recorded time as milliseconds since January 1, 1970). So, we have a constant, MSECDAY, which contains the number of milliseconds in a day. The only change to the constructor is to raise the transaction isolation level to serializable (lines 9–10). This prevents other transactions from interfering with our actions and is the strongest protection a database can provide from outside influences.

All of the new work of the program is performed inside the recheck() method. The TransactionTableModel extends UpdateTableModel, which allows tapes to be checked back in by selecting a tape from a list on the screen. Therefore, the recheck() method also accepts an integer parameter that determines the tape to be rechecked by the user. The first step in the method is to call *setAutoCommit( )* with the value of *false,* meaning that the application will be responsible for determining when the transaction will commit. This method also begins the transaction within the database itself.

Line 19 creates a distinct *Statement* object from the one used by JDBC2TableModel and its descendents. Some driver/database combinations do not allow multiple *Statements* per

Connection object, and creating this one will either generate an exception or close the first one. However, the Oracle driver we are using here does allow it. With this local *Statement*, we create a *ResultSet* containing exactly one value, the next value to be put into the database as the primary key for the Orders table.

If this local *ResultSet* is empty, then there are no rows in the Orders table, so we exit with an error message to the command line (lines 22–25). If the local *ResultSet* does contain a value, we can prepare to insert a new row into the Orders table. First we need the OrderNumber from the local *ResultSet*, so we get it in line 26. The CustomerID is the same as the one for the selected row, since the customer is rechecking the tape. We retrieve that value using the getValueAt( ) method, defined in JDBC2TableModel. Similarly, we can pull the value for the tape ID with the same method, in lines 29–30. The fourth field we need is the due date. In line 31 we create a java.util.Date( ) object for "today." Then, in lines 32–33 we create a java.sql.Date( ) object for "five days from today." We can only insert java.sql.Date objects into the database with the *setDate( )* method, so we must make the conversion here. The fifth value that we will insert into the row is the character string "O" to represent that a tape is checked out. We can do that directly in the insert methods.

Line 34 contains the key method for inserting rows through *ResultSets*. We move the cursor to a nonexistent row with the method *moveToInsertRow( )*. We can now update this row much as we could any other row, except that no current values exist. The OrderNumber, CustomerID, and TapeID fields are updated with calls to the *updateInt( )* method in lines 35–37. We use the *updateDate( )* method to set the new due date, and *updateString( )* to place the value of "O" in the Status field. In all cases, the methods take two parameters. The first is the column number (starting with 1), and the second is the value.

Once the values are set, *insertRow( )* (line 40) is called to insert the row into the database. The cursor is still pointing at an invalid row, so it is important to move it to a valid row after performing the insert. Line 41 moves the cursor to the first row in the *ResultSet*. This completes the first part of the two-step process for rechecking a tape. The second part is to update the previous record of the tape rental to reflect it being returned. Since this is exactly what is accomplished in the update( ) method defined in UpdateTableModel, we call it to complete the task. Since the method is still within the bounds of the transaction started by line 17, any actions performed by the update( ) method will also be part of the transaction. Specifically, the insertion performed in recheck( ) will only be committed to the database if both the update and the insertion are successful. If all goes well, line 43 commits both updates.

Line 44 restores the database to autoCommit mode. This allows any parts of the program that did not explicitly commit their operations to still execute correctly. This does mean that wrapping recheck( ) inside another transaction might not execute as expected. If there are any problems with the execution of the program, an exception will be thrown. In the catch clause at lines 45–50, the transaction is aborted. This means that all changes attempted by the transaction will be removed from the database. Again, autoCommit will be restored at the end of the method.

The class example to interface with the TransactionTableModel is called TransactionJDBC. This class displays a list of tapes checked out by a customer. If a tape is selected from the list and the recheck button is clicked, the database will be updated to show that the customer has rechecked the video.

TransactionJDBC

```
1   import java.sql.*;
2   import javax.swing.*;
3   import java.awt.event.*;
4   import java.util.*;
5
6   public class TransactionJDBC extends TableModelJDBC2 {
7       TransactionTableModel ttm = null;
8
9       public static void main(String args[]) {
10          TransactionJDBC tran = new TransactionJDBC("Updates with Transactions");
11          tran.show();
12          tran.pack();
13      }
14
15      public TransactionJDBC(String title) {
16          super(title);
17          inputButton.setText("Recheck"); // from GUIJDBC
18          ttm = new TransactionTableModel();
19          Vector headVector = new Vector(4);
20          headVector.addElement("Order Number");
21          headVector.addElement("Customer ID");
22          headVector.addElement("Tape ID");
23          headVector.addElement("Due Date");
24          ttm.setHeading(headVector); // from JDBCTableModel
25          dataTable.setSelectionMode(ListSelectionModel.SINGLE_SELECTION);
26          dataTable.setModel(ttm); //dataTable from JTableJDBC
27      }
28
29      public void actionPerformed(ActionEvent evt) {
30          if (evt.getSource() == inputButton) {
31              int item = dataTable.getSelectedRow();
32              if (item!=-1) {
33                  ttm.recheck(item);
34                  dataTable.clearSelection();
35              }
36          }
37          getResultSet();
38      }
39
40      public void getResultSet() {
41          String query = "Select OrderNumber, CustomerID, TapeID, " +
42              "DueDate, Status " +
43              "From Orders " +
44              "Where Status ='0' and " +
45              "CustomerID= " + inputText.getText().trim(); // from GUIJDBC
```

```
46            ttm.showQuery(query); // from JDBC2TableModel
47            dataTableScrollPane.setViewportView(dataTable); // from JTableJDBC
48        }
49
50        public void exitWindow(int i) {
51            ttm.closeConnection();
52            System.exit(i);
53        }
54    }
```

TransactionJDBC

The interface portion of the example follows the same pattern as the rest of the examples. A TransactionTableModel object is declared, and the main() method starts and displays the TransactionJDBC object. In the constructor, we rename the input components as needed and set up the headings for the *JTable*. As with the update example (see Section 4.3), we set the *ListSelectionModel* to single selection so that only one tape can be rechecked at a time.

The actionPerformed() method in lines 29–38 determines the selected row and passes it to the TransactionTableModel in the recheck() method. It calls the getResultSet() method to show the results of applying the update right away. The getResultSet() method in lines 40–48 creates a string with the query, passes that to the showQuery() method to build a *ResultSet* for the TableModel, and then places the new *JTable* in the *JScrollPane* so that we can see the results. The last method signals the TransactionTableModel when the window is closed and exits the program.

5.4   BLOBs

Not too long ago, database systems only handled alphanumeric data. However, as computers have raced into an era of sights and sounds, databases have been dragged along. Now most databases provide support for multimedia data. JDBC provides access to this data through the *Blob* interface. *BLOB* stands for "binary large object," and can be anything from images to sounds to executable files. Since our code is based on the e-commerce application for eVid, we're going to use images as an example of BLOB data.

The first step in getting an image from the database is getting the BLOB. Not surprisingly, this is accomplished with the *ResultSet* method *getBlob()*, which is performed just like any other *getXXX()* method. For example, if the image is the third column,

```
Blob b = rs.getBlob(3);
```

will set the value of b to the BLOB in the database.

There is one very important difference between BLOBs and other types, such as integers. Specifically, the *getBlob()* method does not pull the binary data from the database, it only returns a handle that can be used to get the data. Since BLOBs can be very large, one of the nice consequences of this delayed retrieval is that unwanted BLOBs don't have to be pulled from the database.

There are two methods to get the data: *getBinaryStream( )* and *getBytes( )*. The *getBinaryStream( )* method should be used if any additional filtering is going to be performed on the data, otherwise the two are equivalent. There is also a *length( )* method, which returns the number of bytes in the BLOB.

Since BLOB data can be anything (code, audio, image, etc.), we have to convert the raw binary data into a more useful Java object. Small images can be built from the BLOB using the *ImageIcon* class. It is very direct to use the *getBytes( )* method of the *Blob* interface to create an *ImageIcon* object by

```
ImageIcon ii = new ImageIcon(b.getBytes(0,(int)b.length()))
```

This automatically creates an *ImageIcon* object from the data stored in the database. Note the type cast of the *length( )* method. Normally, the method returns a *long.* This example assumes the size of the BLOB is not too large for the *ImageIcon.*

We can also write binary data to the database with the *Blob* interface. However, since BLOB data is not uniformly treated across database/driver combinations, different syntaxes are needed for different combinations. For example, Oracle defines the field as "blob," but requires a special Oracle method called "empty_blob( )" when creating a *PreparedStatement* to insert a row into the Title table (which contains a field for storing an image associated with a movie). The *prepareStatement( )* would look like

```
outPStmt = outDBConnect.prepareStatement(
                    "insert into Titles values (?,?,?,?,?, empty_blob())");
```

On the other hand, a PostgreSQL database does not require any special method to insert the row, but the table must be defined with a special type called "oid." Eventually, the use of BLOB data will be so common, there will be a standard interface with databases. Combining the two—a BLOB data type and no special functions—would be a good start.

The program example using BLOB data is called BlobJDBC.java. It is a simple search engine to return titles and images of movies. The user enters a keyword, and the *JTable* contains the matches. BlobJDBC uses a *TableModel* called "BlobTableModel." As usual, we will examine the *TableModel* first.

BlobTableModel

```
1   import java.util.*;
2
3   public class BlobTableModel extends JDBCTableModel {
4
5       public BlobTableModel() {
6           super();
7       }
8
```

```
9      public Class getColumnClass(int columnIndex) {
10         if (dataVector.size() == 0) { // from JDBCTableModel
11             return this.getClass();
12         } else {
13             Vector rowVector = (Vector)dataVector.elementAt(0);
14             if (columnIndex > rowVector.size()) { return this.getClass(); }
15             else {
16                 return rowVector.elementAt(columnIndex).getClass();
17             }
18         }
19     }
20  }
```

BlobTableModel

BlobTableModel extends JDBCTableModel and uses the majority of its methods. The only new component is the method getColumnClass( ), which is part of the *AbstractTableModel* class. The default execution of this class is to return a *String,* so that the *JTable* will use the *toString( )* method to represent the elements. In order to display nonalphanumeric data, the *JTable* needs to know the class of the object.

The JDBCTableModel displays the contents of dataVector, a *Vector* of *Vectors.* Each element in each subvector is displayed in a box within the *JTable.* Each column in the *JTable* represents the same attribute in the database, so all of the elements in the column should be the same Java type. Therefore, the getColumnClass( ) first determines if there are any elements in the dataVector in line 10. If there are none, then nothing will be displayed in the *JTable.* Therefore, the class returned by getColumnClass( ) is unimportant, and it returns *this* class, which is BlobTableModel. If there is an element in dataVector, then there must an element at location 0. We use this row to determine the class for each of the corresponding columns. Line 13 retrieves the *Vector* for the first row. Then line 16 returns the class of the element in the first row that corresponds to the columnIndex parameter. In other words, the class of the first element is returned for the first column, and so on. If the columnIndex is too large, then BlobTableModel is returned as the class again.

BlobJDBC is the class example that provides the user interface for the search engine. The program searches for a string in the titles of all of the videos. The search is case sensitive, but all matching substrings will be returned. Figure 5.1 is a captured screen shot of the interface.

BlobJDBC

```
1  import java.sql.*;
2  import javax.swing.*;
3  import java.awt.event.*;
4  import java.util.*;
5
```

```
 6  public class BlobJDBC extends JTableJDBC {
 7      BlobTableModel btm = null;
 8
 9      public static void main(String args[]) {
10          BlobJDBC bJDBC = new BlobJDBC("Graphic JDBC Program w/BLOBs");
11          bJDBC.show();
12          bJDBC.pack();
13      }
14
15      public BlobJDBC(String title) {
16          super(title);
17          btm = new BlobTableModel();
18          Vector headVector = new Vector(2);
19          headVector.addElement("Title");
20          headVector.addElement("Picture");
21          btm.setHeading(headVector); // from JDBCTableModel
22          inputLabel.setText("Search String"); // from GUIJDBC
23          dataTable.setRowHeight(160); // from JTableJDBC
24          dataTable.setModel(btm); // from JTableJDBC
25      }
26
27      public void actionPerformed(ActionEvent evt) {
28          String query = "Select Title, Image " +
29              "From Titles " +
30              "Where Titles.Title like '%" +
31              inputText.getText().trim()+ "%'"; //from GUIJDBC
32
33          ConnectionJDBC CJ = new ConnectionJDBC();
34          Connection dbConnect = null;
35          Statement dbStatement = null;
36          ResultSet dbRS = null;
37          try {
38              dbConnect =
39                  CJ.makeConnection("org.postgresql.Driver",
40                                    "jdbc:postgresql://rbi.baylor.edu/jdbc_book",
41                                    "jdbc_user","guest");\
42              dbConnect.setAutoCommit(false);
43              dbStatement = dbConnect.createStatement();
44              dbRS = dbStatement.executeQuery(query);
45              presentResultSet(dbRS);
46              dbConnect.commit();
47          } catch (SQLException sqlex) {
48              JOptionPane.showMessageDialog(null,sqlex.getMessage());
49          }
50          finally {
51              CJ.closeConnection(dbConnect,dbStatement);
52          }
53      }
```

```
54
55      public void presentResultSet(ResultSet rs)
56          throws SQLException {
57          Vector dataVector = new Vector();
58          if (!rs.next()) JOptionPane.showMessageDialog(null,"No Titles match search.");
59          else {
60              do {
61                  Vector rowVector = new Vector();
62                  rowVector.addElement(rs.getString("Title"));
63                  Blob b = rs.getBlob("image");
64                  rowVector.addElement(new ImageIcon(b.getBytes(0,(int)b.length())));
65                  dataVector.addElement(rowVector);
66                  } while (rs.next());
67          }
68          btm.setData(dataVector);
69          dataTableScrollPane.setViewportView(dataTable); //from JTableJDBC
70      }
71  }
```

BlobJDBC

BlobJDBC starts with the standard construct of defining a *TableModel* object, in this case a BlobTableModel one, and a simple main program that creates the BlobJDBC object and displays it. The constructor in lines 15–25 is also not surprising. It creates the headings with a *Vector* and sets the headings of the *JTable* with the setHeading( ) method. Then, the label for the input field is changed to indicate the desired input. Line 23 uses a new method in the *JTable* class, called *setRowHeight( )*. This increases the height of each row. The default value is 16, but we need more space for our images. The last line of the constructor assigns the BlobTableModel to the *JTable*.

The actionPerformed( ) method (lines 27–53) is also slightly different from our other examples. The query uses the phrase

```
like '%keyword%'
```

in line 31 to indicate that all titles with the keyword appearing anywhere in it should be returned. Lines 39–41 set up the ConnectionJDBC object with the PostgreSQL driver. We use PostgreSQL in this example since it requires no database-specific methods to access BLOB data. There is one small oddity due to PostgreSQL in line 42. PostgreSQL requires that all access to BLOB data be done within a transaction, so we must turn off the autoCommit mode. Once we present the *ResultSet*, we commit the transaction in line 46. As usual, we display an error message if there is a problem, and we disconnect from the database.

Lines 55–70 perform the interesting work in this example, since it converts the *ResultSet*, complete with binary data, into a *Vector* of *Vectors* to be displayed by the BlobTableModel. For each row in the *ResultSet*, we create a new *Vector* with two elements. The first element is pulled straight from the *ResultSet* in line 62. The second element is a BLOB object and is retrieved in a

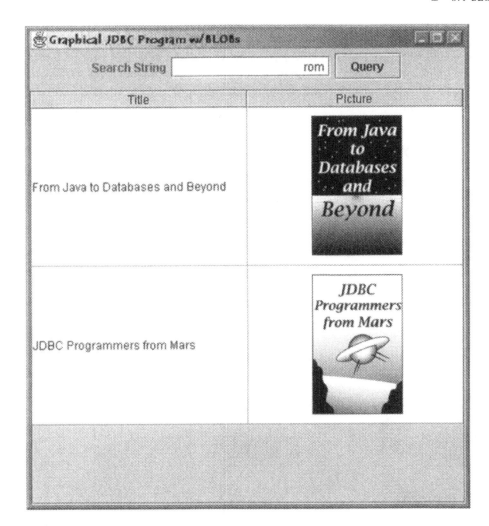

Figure 5.1: Displaying images from database into *JTables.*

two-step process. Step 1 is get the BLOB from the *ResultSet* in line 63. Step 2 is the complicated line 64. First, notice the *length( )* method of the *BLOB* class to determine the size of the object. Next, the *getBytes( )* method brings the binary data to the Java program. The data is retrieved into a buffer used to create a new *ImageIcon* object. This *ImageIcon* object is then added to the *Vector* as the second element. Finally, the completed subvector is added to the collection of vectors, and the process is repeated until no rows remain in the *ResultSet.*

The created *Vector* of *Vectors* is then sent to the BlobTableModel with the setData( ) method. If no rows are in the *ResultSet*, an error message is displayed and an empty *Vector* of *Vectors* is passed to the BlobTableModel. Finally, the dataTable is set to the view of the *JScrollPane*, and the results of the search are visible (see Figure 5.1).

The BLOB data type is one example of what are called *SQL3* data types. Other examples are *character large objects* (CLOB), which can hold large amounts of text data, and *ARRAY,* which holds an array of values in one field. These data types are accessed in much the same way as BLOB data. Subtle differences can be picked up by examining the Java 2 Standard Edition, version 1.3 documentation.

5.5   API Summary

In this chapter, four distinct topics have been covered: drivers, metadata, transactions, and BLOBs. The primary classes, interfaces, and methods are

- *ResultSetMetaData*
  - *getColumnLabel(int ColumnNumber)*
  - *getColumnCount( )*
- *Connection*
  - *commit( )*
  - *rollback( )*
  - *getTransactionIsolation( )*
  - *setTransactionIsolation(int TransationIsolationLevel)*
- *ResultSet*
  - *getBlob( )*
- *Blob*
  - *length( )*
  - *getBytes( )*

5.6   Going Beyond

1. MetaDataJDBC uses the simple approach of pushing all of the values returned from the database into strings. This works for many basic types of data. In order to determine the actual objects being returned, use the *ResultSetMetaData* interface method *getColumn-ClassName( )* to see the Java class being returned by the *getObject( )* method.

2. Extend the MetaDataJDBC so that BLOB objects can be returned as well. Either save the binary data to a file, or use a GUI to display the image.

3. Transaction processing can have a big impact on database operations. Create a program that updates some item in the database and will not commit changes until the user clicks a button. Run two instances of this class at the same time. Change the isolation levels to all that are supported by your driver/database system and note the different possible results.

4. Use JDBCTableModel instead of BlobTableModel with BlobJDBC. What is the result?

chapter **6**

An E-commerce Example

The goal for this guide is to provide the basics needed to connect a database to a Java program. Of course, the best examples of Java programs are the ones that operate on the Internet, so I need to show how JDBC can be used in Internet applications, specifically e-commerce. I briefly discuss applets, then move on to the more realistic multitiered environment.

6.1 Applets

The most obvious use of Java on the Internet is in *applets*—small Java programs that are executed in a browser. However, JDBC programs are not toys, and there are problems with using JDBC in an applet environment. One category of these problems deals with security, and another deals with technical issues.

6.1.1 Security Problems with Applets

The biggest problem with using JDBC in applets is security. First, since one of the restrictions on applets is that they cannot access any machine other than the one from which they were downloaded, the database and the web server have to be on the same machine. Clearly, this is a dangerous situation, as the web server machine is designed to have unknown users access it at all times, while the database must be protected from malicious (or even careless) users.

Second, all of the examples presented in this guide contain the URL of the database, usernames, and passwords needed to make a connection to the database. Although some protection of these services is possible (making the user enter a username and password), it is not possible to hide the names of tables and attributes used to make queries. Thus, information about the database has to be downloaded whenever an applet is requested.

Combining these two issues, we see that using JDBC in an applet allows unknown users to download information about the database, including its location and how to access it. This

73

means that any JDBC applet deployment should only be in restricted environments, such as in-house applications.

6.1.2   Technical Issues with Applets

Even without the security concerns, there are technical reasons why applets are not a good choice for JDBC. Another restriction on applets is that they cannot use what are called *native methods*—that is, methods that access the client computer directly. Although that doesn't appear to be a problem, the Sun JDBC-ODBC bridge driver does use native methods, as do all Type 1 and Type 2 drivers. Again, in-house applications can solve this problem by placing the needed software on each machine, but general use is limited to Type 3 or Type 4 drivers, such as the examples in Sections 4.3 and 5.4.

However, even these drivers have some problems when used with an applet. Within the JDBC API, many of the important classes are actually defined as interfaces. Thus, it is the responsibility of the driver to instantiate the class. Since Type 3 and Type 4 drivers are pure Java, they must contain the code for the instantiation in a jar file. Unfortunately, driver jar files tend to be very large as compared to the size of an applet. For example, the PostgreSQL jar file we're using in the examples is over 193,000 bytes, while a JDBC applet will usually be less than 10,000 bytes. This is a significant problem, even in the days of high-speed Internet connections.

All that aside, applets are a powerful interface tool for the user. We would like to take advantage of this tool by modeling our Internet application like the example in Section 2.3. In that example, the JDBC classes were all managed in the *TableModel* class, while the interface program managed the *JTable* and communicated with the *TableModel* class with *Strings* and *Vectors*.

The equivalent notion in the Internet application world is to have a program at the server that handles the JDBC part of the code, and an applet that handles the interface. The two programs communicate by sending *Strings* and *Vectors* to each other. Within the Internet computing environment, server-side programs are called *servlets*.

6.2   Servlets

Servlets extend our analogy from Chapter 1 by changing the point of interaction with users. In our original analogy, we assume the store is the point where customers arrive to purchase goods. However, with servlets, a better analogy is to picture a large sales force spread throughout the country, contacting potential customers. These agents come back to the store to pick up merchandise, and then deliver it to customers (see Figure 6.1).

The agents represent web pages downloaded by the user. The user can interact with an agent, but cannot interact with the database without going through the agent. This solves the problems of using JDBC with applets. The agent, either HTML or an applet, does not require the heavy JDBC jar files, so it loads quickly. The database is accessed through a servlet, so the tight security restrictions of applets are lifted. Thus, the database can be on any machine, eliminating some security risks.

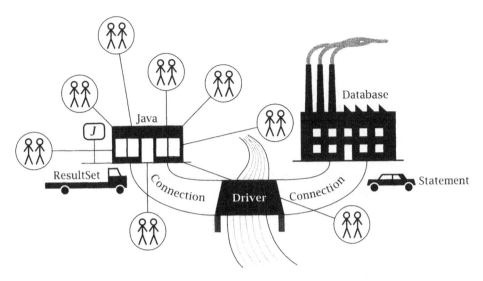

Figure 6.1: Analogy with servlets and HTML pages.

To fully discuss using servlets would require a book at least as long as this one, so this guide cannot cover servlets in significant detail. The information provided here is enough to get started, but it leaves out many issues. To better understand servlets, see [5]. The guide's web site contains instructions for setting up tomcat, a commonly used, free servlet engine.

In order to use servlets, we have to have a servlet engine available. The servlet engine can either stand alone or be integrated into a web server. The best approach is to use a stand-alone servlet engine for development and testing, then use an integrated servlet engine for production. This helps minimize the problems with taking an application online.

In either case, the servlet engine receives requests much like a web server. In fact, stand-alone servlet engines typically respond to web requests by using port 8080. The URL for such requests looks exactly like a URL for a web page, except that we have to specify the port number. For example, to connect to a servlet named ServletHTML running on the local host, we use the URL

```
http://localhost:8080/servlet/QueryServletJDBC
```

The "servlet" in the URL is only a directory name and does not signify anything special. However, it is a common default directory name for servlets. This directory is the location for QueryServletJDBC class, a Java class designed to be a servlet. When the request is received by the servlet engine, it loads the desired class and executes it, much like a web browser loading an applet.

Since our servlet also connects to a database via JDBC, the driver jar file must also be accessible to the servlet engine. Usually, there is a specific directory where the servlet engine looks for such jar files. Clearly, the easiest thing to do is copy the driver jar file to that directory.

When the servlet engine executes our JDBC-aware class, it will look in that directory to load the driver class.

The servlet API consists of the packages javax.servlet and javax.servlet.http. However, we can examine the crucial components of the API by looking at the abstract class *HttpServlet*. The class provides default implementations for several of the common methods used by servlets. In this respect, it is similar to the *AbstractTableModel* we use in Sections 2.3 and 4.3. In order to use the *HttpServlet* class, we must override at least one method. The most common choices to override are *doGet()* and *doPost()*.

doGet() Method.   The *doGet()* method is called whenever the servlet engine receives a GET request. This is the typical request issued by a web browser, and it can also be requested by a form or an applet. The *doGet()* method accepts two parameters: an *HttpServletRequest* (usually called *req*) and an *HttpServletResponse* (usually called *res*). The *HttpServletRequest* is an interface for bringing information from the client to the servlet, specifically the method *getInputStream()* for reading binary data and *getReader()* for reading character data. Conversely, *HttpServletResponse* is for sending information to the client from the servlet. It contains the methods *getOutputStream()* and *getWriter()* for writing binary and character data, respectively. For example, if we want to write an HTML page as a result of calling the servlet, we can create a *PrintWriter* object as

```
PrintWriter pw = res.getWriter();
```

We can then use *PrintWriter* methods to create the HTML page, such as

```
pw.println("<title>JDBC Using Servlets</title>");
```

which would add a title to the HTML page.

doPost Method.   The *doPost()* method accepts the same parameters as the *doGet()* method. The *doPost()* method replies to applets or forms using the "POST" action. The primary difference between a GET and a POST is that GET actions send information in the URL field, while POST actions use the body of the http request. As a result, GET actions are usually limited in length, while POST actions can be as long as desired. It is also the case that GET requests are visible to the user, since the information is in the URL, while POST requests are not. Finally, only character data can be sent via the GET action, while POST can carry binary data as well.

init() and destroy() Methods.   In addition to the *doGet()* and *doPost()* methods, two other important parts of the *HttpServlet* class are the *init()* and *destroy()* methods. The *init()* method is called when the servlet engine loads the servlet, much like the *init()* method of an applet is called when the applet is loaded by the web browser. The *init()* method is for initializing any resources that might be held during the lifetime of the servlet, such as *Drivers*, or sometimes *Connections*. The *destroy()* method is called whenever the servlet engine exits, or when the servlet must be terminated for some reason. The resources reserved in the *init()* method should be released in the *destroy()* method.

Recall from our analogy that our business has many agents, but only one store. This analogy holds for servlets as well. Many web browsers can request information from the servlet, but there is only one servlet to respond. This means that any class variables used within the servlet (such as *Connection, ResultSet,* etc.) will be accessed by every requesting thread. Servlets must be very careful with respect to synchronization issues.

Finally, although the servlet API is part of J2EE, Sun's Java 2 Enterprise Edition, it is not part of Sun's Java 2 Standard Edition version 1.3. Therefore, if we are using the standard edition, we have to download and install the servlet API. This API must be used in the classpath of javac. This means that the appropriate values in an integrated development environment (IDE) must be set, or the command line compilation must look like

```
javac –classpath servlet.jar QueryServletJDBC.java
```

The servlet API is also needed in order to execute the class, but the servlet engine already contains it, or has the API in its directory of libraries.

6.3 **Multitiered Architecture Example**

One of the advantages of a multitiered system is that we can solve problems at three different levels. We can handle data presentation with an applet, business logic with a servlet, and database access with PL/SQL. The only important issue is how to communicate between the components. Communication between the servlet and the database is exactly the same as in Section 3.2, where we use *CallableStatements*. On the other hand, communication between the applet and the servlet is not obvious, so I'll start here.

The applet sends information to the servlet using the HTTP protocol. Essentially, it constructs the URL of the servlet, including parameters. This invokes the *doGet()* method in the servlet. The servlet sends information back to the applet via a binary socket connection. This allows the servlet to send serialized objects to the applet, which greatly increases the sophistication of the reply. Unfortunately, it also means that only objects that support the *Serializable* interface can be sent this way. Specifically, this means that *ResultSet* objects *cannot* be sent. However, since we can use *JTable* displays based on *Vectors* instead of *ResultSets*, and *Vectors* are serializable if all of their elements are serializable, we can use the techniques from examples like that in Section 2.4.

In order to simplify the applet code, a class called Communication exists to handle the basic issues. The source code, called Communication.java, is available in the Appendix, but discussion of the specifics is beyond the scope of this text.

6.3.1 The Applet

The code for the applet is found on the web site as ServletApplet.java. From a JDBC perspective, this program is very simple, as it does not even import the java.sql package. However, this class implements the user interface for our multitiered example, and it communicates with the servlet. This example is also rather lengthy for a text, so the discussion is split into two parts.

ServletApplet Part 1

```
1   import java.awt.*;
2   import java.awt.event.*;
3   import java.io.*;
4   import java.text.*;
5   import java.util.*;
6   import java.net.*;
7   import javax.swing.*;
8   import javax.swing.event.*;
9   import javax.swing.table.*;
10
11  public class ServletApplet extends JApplet
12      implements ActionListener  {
13      BlobTableModel btm = new BlobTableModel();
14      Communication cServlet = new Communication();
15
16      JLabel keywordLabel = new JLabel("Movie Title Keyword");
17      JTextField keywordText = new JTextField(" ",15);
18      JButton keywordButton = new JButton("Search");
19      JButton moreButton = new JButton("More");
20      JButton orderButton = new JButton("Order");
21      JPanel keywordPanel = new JPanel(new FlowLayout(FlowLayout.CENTER,5,5));
22      JTable dataTable = new JTable();
23      JScrollPane dataTableScrollPane = new JScrollPane();
24
25      StringBuffer keyword = null;
26      Integer next = null;
27
28      public void init() {
29          keywordLabel.setLabelFor(keywordText);
30          keywordText.addActionListener(this);
31          keywordButton.addActionListener(this);
32          orderButton.addActionListener(this);
33          moreButton.addActionListener(this);
34          moreButton.setEnabled(false);
35
36          keywordPanel.add(keywordLabel);
37          keywordPanel.add(keywordText);
38          keywordPanel.add(keywordButton);
39          keywordPanel.add(moreButton);
40          keywordPanel.add(orderButton);
41
42          Vector headingsVector = new Vector(3);
43          headingsVector.addElement(new String("Title"));
44          headingsVector.addElement(new String("Price"));
45          headingsVector.addElement(new String("Cover"));
```

```
46          btm.setHeading(headingsVector);
47
48          dataTable.setModel(btm);
49          dataTable.setRowHeight(160);
50          dataTable.setSelectionMode(ListSelectionModel.SINGLE_SELECTION);
51
52          dataTableScrollPane.setViewportView(dataTable);
53
54          getContentPane().setLayout(new BorderLayout(5,5));
55          getContentPane().add("North",keywordPanel);
56          getContentPane().add("Center",dataTableScrollPane);
57      }
58
59      public void start() {
60          getContentPane().validate();
61          repaint();
62      }
63
64      public void actionPerformed(ActionEvent evt) {
65          if ( evt.getSource() == keywordText ||
66               evt.getSource() == keywordButton ) {
67            keyword=new StringBuffer("%");
68            keyword.append(keywordText.getText().trim());
69            keyword.append("%");
70            next = showQuery(keyword.toString(), new Integer(1));
71          }
72          if (evt.getSource() == moreButton ) {
73            next = showQuery(keyword.toString(), next);
74          }
75          if (evt.getSource() == orderButton ) {
76              int choice = dataTable.getSelectedRow();
77              if (choice > -1) {
78                  placeOrder(choice);
79              } else {
80                  JOptionPane.
81                      showMessageDialog(null,"Select a video before ordering.");
82              }
83          }
84          dataTable.clearSelection();
85          if (next.intValue() > 1) {
86              moreButton.setEnabled(true);
87          } else {
88              moreButton.setEnabled(false);
89          }
90  }
```

ServletApplet Part 1

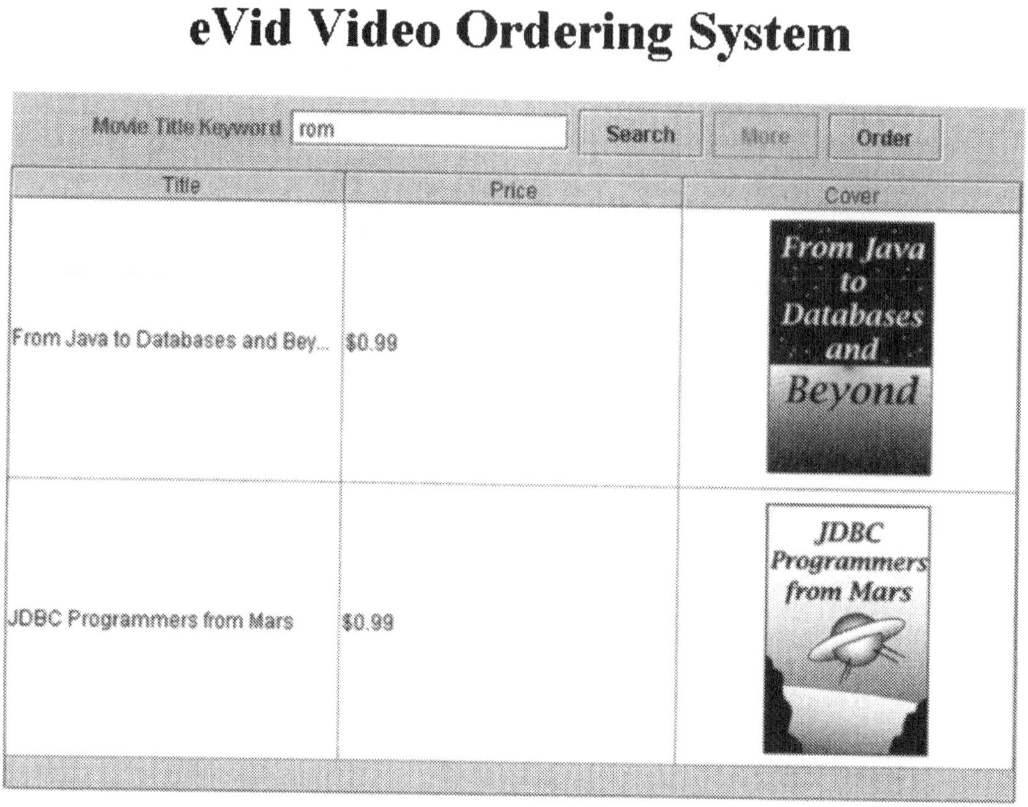

eVid Video Ordering System

Figure 6.2: Screen shot of applet for orders.

The ServletApplet example does not use the GUIJDBC class found in the other examples because the interface is more complex. It does use the BlobTableModel from Section 5.4 because it presents *JTables* with BLOB data to the user. It also uses the Communication class found on the web site.

The interface has five input components, all grouped into one panel. The components are listed as data members in lines 16–20. The first is a label for text input, then next is a *JTextField* to allow the user to input a keyword for searches. Line 18 declares the button to be pressed when the user wants to search the database, while line 19 contains a button labeled "More." This button will be active when the number of search results is too large to present at one time to the user. Line 20 creates a button so a user can order a tape. All of these components are placed in the panel defined in line 21. Lines 22 and 23 are the familiar dataTable and dataTableScrollPane we use in all of the *JTable* examples. A screen shot of the interface appears in Figure 6.2.

ServletApplet also contains two data members used to perform the query. The first is a *StringBuffer* called "keyword" that will hold the search value entered by the user. The second is an Integer (not int) called "next." If the search yields a very large result, it will be split into multiple requests. The variable next holds the relative row number for the start of subsequent requests.

Like all applets, this one requires an *init()* method, which is performed when the applet is loaded into the browser. There are many similarities between this example and BlobJDBC in Section 5.4. However, in this case, we do not use the default behavior of GUIJDBC to handle some of the GUI details. First, the applet registers itself as a listener for all of its buttons and the text field (lines 30-33), although one small difference is that the "More" button is disabled at the beginning (line 34). All of the components for the user input are added to a panel called "keywordPanel" (lines 36-40). The headings for the BlobTableModel are set by creating a *Vector* of *Strings* in lines 42-45 and using the setHeading() method in line 46. The *JTable* is assigned an *AbstractTableModel* (line 48). The default row height is increased to 160 in line 49 to accommodate images in the *JTable*. The selection mode is set as in UpdateJDBC (see Section 4.3). The *JTable* is added to the *JScrollPane* (line 52). Finally, the layout of the *JApplet* is set and all of the components are added to the content pane of the *JApplet*, in lines 54-56.

The start() method is invoked whenever the user returns to this page, or after the init() method. It does very little for the applet. Whenever it is invoked, it simply validates all of the components to make sure they have the correct values, and then repaints the screen. The actionPerformed() method is triggered whenever the user clicks on one of the buttons or hits enter in the keyword text field. There are three buttons and one text field in the keywordPanel, so we have four possible executions here. Lines 65-70 handle the case if the keywordButton is clicked or the user hits the enter key in the keywordText field. In either case, a query is generated. The keyword is pulled from the keywordText field, wildcards are added to it, and the showQuery() method is called. This method is similar to the showQuery() method in JDBC2TableModel. In that case, the query string is passed to the *TableModel*. Here, we do the same thing, only the communication is more complex. The third possible input from the user is clicking the "More" button. This button is enabled only if the servlet indicates that there are more values to be returned for this query. As such, the same keyword is sent to the showQuery() method, but with a higher value for the row to be returned by the query. The final input from a user is to click the "Order" button. We follow a path similar to TransactionJDBC (see Section 5.3) of extracting the row selected by the user and sending that value to a method similar to recheck() in TransactionJDBC. This time the method is called placeOrder(). In any event, any selected values are cleared after receiving the new values from the database. If there are more values in the query than can be displayed, the "More" button is enabled; otherwise it is disabled (lines 85-89).

ServletApplet Part 2

```
92    private Integer showQuery(String keyword, Integer next) {
93        try {
94            cServlet.
95                setString("http://localhost:8080/servlet/QueryServletJDBC");
96            cServlet.addParam("keyword",keyword);
97            cServlet.addParam("start",next.toString());
98            cServlet.connect();
```

```
 99            next = (Integer)cServlet.readObject();
100            if (next.intValue()==-1) {
101                JOptionPane.showMessageDialog(null,"No titles found.");
102                return new Integer(1);
103            }
104            else {
105                Vector dataVector = (Vector)cServlet.readObject();
106                for (int i=0; i<dataVector.size(); i++) {
107                    Vector v = (Vector)dataVector.elementAt(i);
108                    String imageURLString =
109                        "http://localhost:8080/jdbc/images/" +
110                        (String)v.elementAt(2);
111                    URL imageURL = new URL(imageURLString);
112                    ImageIcon image = new ImageIcon(imageURL);
113                    v.setElementAt(image,2);
114                }
115                btm.setData(dataVector);
116                dataTableScrollPane.setViewportView(dataTable);
117            }
118        } catch (Exception e) {
119            JOptionPane.
120                showMessageDialog(null,"Problem with the data. Try again.");
121        } finally { try {cServlet.disconnect();} catch (IOException ioex) {} }
122        return next;
123    }
124
125    private void placeOrder(int choice) {
126        try {
127            cServlet.
128                setString("http://localhost:8080/servlet/UpdateServletJDBC");
129            cServlet.addParam("title",(String)btm.getValueAt(choice,0));
130            cServlet.addParam("customer",
131                              JOptionPane.showInputDialog("Enter Customer ID"));
132            cServlet.connect();
133            Integer returnValue = (Integer)cServlet.readObject();
134            if (returnValue.intValue() == 0) {
135                JOptionPane.
136                    showMessageDialog(null,"Thank you for ordering " +
137                                       (String)btm.getValueAt(choice,0));
138            } else if (returnValue.intValue() == -1) {
139                JOptionPane.showMessageDialog(null,"Invalid Customer ID");
140            } else if (returnValue.intValue() == -2) {
141                JOptionPane.
142                    showMessageDialog(null,"There are no copies of " +
143                                       (String)btm.getValueAt(choice,0) +
144                                       " available. Please try again.");
145            } else {
```

```
146                 JOptionPane.
147                     showMessageDialog(null,"There was a problem with "
148                                     + "your order.  Please try again.");
149             }
150         } catch (Exception e) {
151             JOptionPane.
152                 showMessageDialog(null,"Problem with the data. Try again.");
153         } finally { try {cServlet.disconnect();} catch (IOException ioex) {}}
154     }
155 }
```

ServletApplet Part 2

The showQuery() method in lines 92–123 handles the communication with the servlet and displays the values returned (using the BlobTableModel). The first four steps of the method set up the connection to the servlet. The setString() method of Communication determines the base URL of the servlet to be called. The addParam() method requires a label and a value. The label is the name of the parameter. The servlet will be able to retrieve the value by asking for the name of the parameter. The connect() method attempts to connect to the servlet and pass the parameters to it.

Once the connection is complete, the applet attempts to read from the servlet using the Communication method readObject(). The applet will block until this method returns. The response from the servlet always contains an integer indicating the status of the query. A value of −1 indicates that no values met the search criteria. Any other value indicates success. A value of 1 not only means success, but also that all found matches are returned. Any other value indicates that there are additional values to be returned.

If no rows are found, the showQuery() displays an error message and returns a value of 1, indicating that no further values are available in the database. If values are found, then these will be returned to the user in the form of a *Vector* of *Vectors*. The applet uses the Communication method readObject() again to read all of the values in one operation (line 105). Then, each element in dataVector (which are *Vectors* themselves) are retrieved. The servlet returns only string values, but for this query, one of those values is the URL of an image to be displayed. Before the data can be displayed correctly by the BlobTableModel, we must convert the URL into an *ImageIcon*.

First, in lines 108–110, we construct the fully qualified URL. Second, in line 111, we create a URL object with this name. Line 112 builds the *ImageIcon* object from the URL. We then replace the string in the *Vector* with the *ImageIcon* object. After updating all of the elements this way, we pass the dataVector to the BlobTableModel and we set the view of the dataTableScrollPane to the new *JTable*. As always, if there is an exception, we display an error message (lines 118–120), and we also always terminate the connection to the Communication object, which closes the input stream.

We can now turn our attention to the part of the applet that updates the database with orders. It is important to realize we are not handling *any* security concerns with this applet.

Table 6.1: Servlet Return Codes

Value	Meaning	Lines Processing
0	success	lines 134–137
–1	invalid CustomerID	lines 138–139
–2	out of tapes	lines 140–144
all others	error condition	lines 145–149

Any production system would need significantly more sophisticated protections in place. These components are omitted in order to focus on the JDBC issues.

We start the placeOrder() method in the same way as the showQuery() method—we set the servlet name in the Communication object by passing in the URL of the servlet, and we pass in the values to be sent to the servlet. The servlet URL is the same machine and directory, but it is UpdateJDBCServlet this time. The parameters for placing an order are the title of the desired video and the ID number of the customer placing the order. The title can be retrieved using the getValueAt() method of our BlobTableModel object. The title is the first field in displayed by the *JTable*, and the parameter passed into the method is the desired row. We cast the *Object* returned by the method into a *String*, and the first parameter is ready. The second parameter is input by the user with the *showInputDialog()* method of the *JOptionPane* class. This method creates a window with an input text field. When the user clicks "OK," the character values in the field are returned by the method.

After the URL is set and the parameters are passed, a connection is made to the servlet. The applet then reads the Integer returned. The possible return values for the servlet are shown in Table 6.1.

In all cases, an appropriate message is displayed using the *showMessageDialog()* method as in our other examples. If any exception occurs, an error message is displayed (lines 150–152), and line 153 disconnects the applet from the servlet.

6.3.2 The Servlet

Let's move to the server side and discuss the servlet. Servlets should respond to only one specific web request. This allows them to be efficient pieces of code. Our applet sends two types of requests: a query for movie titles and an update for placing an order. This means we need two servlet classes. The one to handle the query is called QueryServletJDBC, while the one for the update is called UpdateServletJDBC.

The purpose of both servlets is to interface with the applet and the database. As such, both have the java.sql package we use in the other examples, and they also communicate with the applet via a direct socket communication. Both servlets are invoked with the GET-style method of the HTTP protocol.

QueryServletJDBC

```
1    import java.io.*;
2    import java.sql.*;
3    import java.text.*;
4    import java.util.*;
5    import javax.servlet.*;
6    import javax.servlet.http.*;
7
8    public class QueryServletJDBC extends HttpServlet {
9        static final int POOLSIZE = 10;
10       static final int LIMIT = 10;
11
12       Connection[] Pool = new Connection[POOLSIZE];
13       boolean[] available = new boolean[POOLSIZE];
14
15       public void init() throws ServletException {
16           super.init();
17           try {
18               Class.forName("oracle.jdbc.driver.OracleDriver");
19               for (int i=0; i<POOLSIZE; i++) {
20                   Pool[i] = DriverManager.getConnection("jdbc:oracle:oci8:@",
                                                          "jdbc_user","guest");
21
22                   available[i]=true;
23               }
24           } catch (Exception ex) {
25           throw new UnavailableException(this,ex.getMessage());
26           }
27       }
28
29       public void destroy() {
30           for (int i=0; i<POOLSIZE; i++) {
31               try {
32                   Pool[i].close();
33               } catch (SQLException sqlex) {}
34           }
35       }
36
37       public void doGet(HttpServletRequest req, HttpServletResponse res)
38           throws ServletException, IOException, UnavailableException {
39           Connection dbConnect  = checkout();
40           if (dbConnect==null) throw new
41               UnavailableException(this,"Too many users. Try again later");
42           PreparedStatement pStmt = null;
43           int count = 1;
44           String keyword = req.getParameter("keyword");
```

```
45        String startCount = req.getParameter("start");
46        ObjectOutputStream os = new ObjectOutputStream(res.getOutputStream());
47
48     if (keyword != null && startCount != null) {
49        try {
50            count = Integer.parseInt(startCount);
51        } catch (Exception e) {count = 1;}
52        try {
53            pStmt = dbConnect.
54                prepareStatement("Select Title, Price, URL " +
55                                 "From Titles " +
56                                 "Where Title like ? ",
57                                 ResultSet.TYPE_SCROLL_INSENSITIVE,
58                                 ResultSet.CONCUR_READ_ONLY);
59            pStmt.setString(1, keyword);
60            ResultSet rs = pStmt.executeQuery();
61            if (!rs.absolute(count)) rs.first();
62            presentResultSet(rs, os);
63        } catch (SQLException sqlex) {
64            os.writeObject(new Integer(-1));
65        } finally {
66            try {pStmt.close();}catch (SQLException sqlex){}
67        }
68     }
69     else {
70        os.writeObject(new Integer(-3));
71     }
72     checkin(dbConnect);
73  }
74
75  private void presentResultSet(ResultSet rs, ObjectOutputStream oos)
76     throws IOException, SQLException {
77     if (rs == null) { oos.writeObject(new Integer(-1)); }
78     else {
79        if (rs.getRow()==0) { oos.writeObject(new Integer(-1)); }
80        else {
81            Vector dataVector = new Vector();
82            int recNumber = 0;
83            do {
84                Vector newRow = new Vector();
85                newRow.addElement(rs.getString("title"));
86                newRow.addElement(NumberFormat.getCurrencyInstance().
87                                  format(new Double(rs.getDouble("price"))));
88                newRow.addElement(rs.getString("url"));
89                dataVector.addElement(newRow);
90            } while (rs.relative(1) && ++recNumber < LIMIT);
91            int count = rs.getRow();
```

```
92                    if (count==0) count=1;
93                    oos.writeObject(new Integer(count));
94                    oos.writeObject(dataVector);
95                }
96            }
97        }
98
99        private synchronized Connection checkout() {
100           int i=0;
101           while (i<10 && !available[i]) i++;
102           if (i<10) {
103               available[i]=false;
104               return Pool[i];
105           } else {
106               return null;
107           }
108       }
109
110       private synchronized void checkin(Connection c) {
111           int i=0;
112           while (Pool[i] != c && i < 10) i++;
113           if (i<10) {
114               available[i]=true;
115           }
116       }
117   }
```

QueryServletJDBC

Every time an applet makes a request of a servlet, the same class is invoked by the servlet engine. As a result, we have to be aware of the possibility that the servlet could be responding to multiple requests at the same time. One option is for the servlet to implement the *SingleThreadModel* interface. This restricts execution to only one thread at a time. In this example, we do not follow that approach, thereby allowing for more scalable systems.

Our first data members are two constants, POOLSIZE and LIMIT. The integer POOLSIZE sets the maximum allowable number of simultaneous connections the servlet can fulfill, while LIMIT is the maximum number of rows per query the servlet will return to the applet. Due to multithreading concerns, we do not have a *Statement* object as a data member. In a multithreaded execution, the data members will be shared by all threads. For example, a *Statement* can only be associated with one *ResultSet*. Whenever a *Statement* performs an *executeQuery()* method, any open *ResultSet* is closed and a new one is opened. Imagine a scenario where a query has retrieved the videos with "Java" in the title, but has not read any of the rows from the *ResultSet*. A second query invokes the servlet, asking for videos with "Programmers" in the title. The *Statement* performs the *executeQuery()* method for

"Programmers." The first execution now resumes. It accesses the *ResultSet*, only to discover that the videos are all wrong.

As a result, in QueryServletJDBC, the only java.sql package data member is an array of *Connections*. This allows a very simple means for sharing *Connections*—by a process called *pooling*. The guide's web site has links to sophisticated *Connection* pooling packages, but here we use a simple means to illustrate the concept. Also, DBMSs have connection pools of their own, which are distinct from this servlet pooling system.

Our connection pool consists of two parallel arrays. One array is of *Connections* (line 12), the other of Booleans (line 13). Whenever a thread tries to execute the servlet, it checks out one of the *Connections* (line 39). Whenever a thread exits the servlet, it checks in the *Connection* (line 72). Since all *Connections* are exactly the same, it doesn't matter to the requesting thread which *Connection* it gets, as long as no other threads are using the same one.

The init() method of the servlet is called when the servlet is first loaded by the servlet engine. It is only called once, no matter how many requests are made of the servlet. Therefore, we don't have to worry about multithreading here. Line 18 loads the Oracle driver into the JVM. This will fail unless the jar file containing the driver is accessible to the servlet engine. Lines 19-23 form a loop to create the *Connection* objects used by the pool. Every time a *Connection* object is created, the corresponding Boolean array value is set to *true*. If there are any problems with the init() method, an *UnavailableException* is thrown. This will prevent the browser from accessing the servlet and usually results in an error message, displayed to the user. The "destroy" method in lines 29-35 is called when the servlet engine is closing. This method simply closes all of the connections to the database.

Every time the servlet is invoked, the doGet() method is called. This method is the focal point for the execution of the servlet and, with the possibility of multithreading, it is even more so the center of our attention. The doGet() method accepts an *HttpServletRequest* parameter (called "req" on line 37) and a *HttpServletResponse* parameter (called "res" on line 37). The parameter req is used to receive additional information from the applet, but in this case there is nothing besides the parameters. However, the parameter res will be used to create the *OutputStream* (from the servlet's perspective) from which the applet will input data.

Since local variables are not shared, the doGet() method defines a local copy of a *Connection* object in line 39, and provides it with the value returned from the checkout() method. Lines 40 and 41 generate another *UnavailableException* if there are no connections available. QueryServletJDBC uses pStmt—a *PreparedStatement*—for queries. Every invocation of the servlet will have its own copy of this variable. The local variable count (line 43) is used to determine the location for future queries, if the *ResultSet* is too big to be sent to the applet.

We are now ready to process the request. The first thing we do is retrieve all of the parameters. In this example, there are two possible parameters, retrieved in lines 44 and 45. If either of the parameters are not present, then the *getParameter()* method will return *null*. Otherwise, it returns the value provided by the addParam() method in the Communication class. The results of the servlet will be passed back to the applet via an *ObjectOutputStream*. Line 46 creates the *ObjectOutputStream* that is associated with the *HttpServletResponse*.

With the input value found and the output steams established, we can now process the request. If either keyword or startCount is null, then the request is not valid (line 48) and we return an *Integer* object with the value of −3 to indicate the error (lines 69-71). If the request is valid, it is processed in lines 49-68. The first step is to convert the *String* startCount to the integer count by using the static *parseInt()* method of the *Integer* class. The startCount parameter indicates the first row to be returned from a *ResultSet*. If there is a problem parsing the data, the default value of 1 is used for count.

Next, in lines 53-58, we create the *PreparedStatement* object pStmt. (See Section 3.1 for details on using *PreparedStatements*.) The *ResultSet* generated by this pStmt will be scrollable but not updatable, and it will not see updates performed by other transactions. With pStmt created, we fill the only placeholder with the keyword passed in from the applet. Note that no attempt is made to add wildcards here. This allows the same query to be used in exact-match cases if desired. In line 60, we execute the query and generate the *ResultSet*. If we are processing a large *ResultSet*, then the startCount passed into the servlet will be greater than 1. However, since the database can change between executions of the applet (and since it is possible to humanly pass the value of the parameter directly in the URL), we check the validity of the value in line 61. If startCount is not in the *ResultSet*, the call to *absolute()* will return *false*. In that case, we set the cursor to the first row in the *ResultSet*. After the check, we move the cursor to the desired row and call presentResultSet(). This time, instead of just passing in the *ResultSet*, we also pass in the *ObjectOutputStream*. If there is an *SQLException*, we send a −1 to the applet. At the end of executing the query, we close pStmt. An *SQLException* can be thrown in this finally block, but since little can be done in this case, we do nothing with it.

Except for a few minor differences dealing with *ObjectOutputStreams*, the presentResultSet() method in lines 75-97 is not different from the other examples where we convert the *ResultSet* into a *Vector* of *Vectors*. This method uses writing a value of −1 to the *ObjectOutputStream* as the equivalent of writing an error message to the screen. We first make sure the *ResultSet* object exists, and if not, we write an error message (line 77). If the *ResultSet* exists but the cursor is not on a valid row, we write an error message (line 79). If everything is OK, then we loop over the elements in the *ResultSet* until either we have processed LIMIT rows, or the *ResultSet* is empty. The test is in line 90. The method *relative()* moves the cursor a given number of rows forward (or backward if the parameter is negative). By passing in 1 as the parameter, this is the same as using the *next()* method.

For each row, the *ResultSet* method *getString()* is used for the title of the video and the URL of its cover. However, the price of the video is stored in the database as a floating point number. We use the method rs.getDouble("price") to retrieve the data. This method returns a double value, not a *Double* object. Since doubles may have more than two decimal places, the output of the application must be formatted so that only two decimal places are displayed. The *NumberFormat* class contains the static method *getCurrencyInstance()*, which returns a *NumberFormat* object designed to output values in a local currency. Once all of the elements in a row are processed, it is added to the *Vector* of *Vectors*.

Once the loop is completed, we check to see if we have reached the end of the *ResultSet*. The *getRow()* method returns the current row number, or 0 if the cursor is not on a valid row. If the cursor is not on a valid row, we have processed the entire *ResultSet* and the next query will need to start at the beginning, so we set the count to 1 in line 92. We then send this value to the applet and follow it with the *Vector* of *Vectors* containing the data.

The last part of the servlet deals with our simplified connection pool. Whenever a request is made to the database, a distinct *Connection* object is returned by the checkout() method in lines 99–108. A parallel array, called Boolean, actually controls the access to the *Connection* object. Note that both the checkout() method and the checkin() method (lines 110–116) are synchronized. This means that no two threads can be in these methods at the same time. However, the rest of the servlet can be multithreaded.

The checkout() method is very simple. It loops through the available array, looking for a value of *true*. If it finds an available *Connection*, it sets the available array entry to *false* and returns the corresponding *Connection* object. If no *Connections* are available, it returns *null*. If the checkout() method is not synchronized, it is possible for two threads to receive the same *Connection*. Many of the assumptions made in the rest of the servlet would then fail, and unpredictable results would follow. The checkin() method is even easier. It accepts a *Connection* object as a parameter and then looks up the *Connection* in the pool. It sets the value of the corresponding Boolean array back to *true*.

The servlet to update the database and allow customers to check out videos is called UpdateServletJDBC. It uses *CallableStatements* to execute stored procedures in the database. The servlet is the place for business logic, and here we demonstrate that by allowing all tapes to be checked out for five days. Changes in this policy would require changing the servlet. Again, this restriction is to demonstrate the types of code that might be in each part of the system. Obviously, production-level software should allow changing the number of days without changing the program.

UpdateServletJDBC

```
1   import java.io.*;
2   import java.sql.*;
3   import java.text.*;
4   import java.util.*;
5   import javax.servlet.*;
6   import javax.servlet.http.*;
7
8   public class UpdateServletJDBC extends HttpServlet {
9       static final long MSECDAY = 86400000L;
10
11      public void doGet(HttpServletRequest req, HttpServletResponse res)
12          throws ServletException, IOException, UnavailableException {
13          String customerStr = req.getParameter("customer");
14          String movie = req.getParameter("title");
15          ConnectionJDBC CJ = new ConnectionJDBC();
16          Connection dbConnect = null;
17          CallableStatement checkOutUpdate = null;
18          ObjectOutputStream os = new ObjectOutputStream(res.getOutputStream());
19
20          if (customerStr != null && movie != null) {
21              try {
22                  dbConnect =
23                      CJ.makeConnection("oracle.jdbc.driver.OracleDriver",
24                                        "jdbc:oracle:oci8:@","jdbc_user","guest");
```

```
25              checkOutUpdate = dbConnect.
26                  prepareCall("{call place_order(?,?,?,?)}");
27              int customerId = Integer.parseInt(customerStr);
28              checkOutUpdate.setInt(1,customerId);
29              checkOutUpdate.setString(2,movie);
30              java.util.Date today = new java.util.Date();
31              java.sql.Date sqlDate = new
32                  java.sql.Date(today.getTime()+5*MSECDAY);
33              checkOutUpdate.setDate(3,sqlDate);
34              checkOutUpdate.registerOutParameter(4,Types.INTEGER);
35              checkOutUpdate.executeUpdate();
36              os.writeObject(new Integer(checkOutUpdate.getInt(4)));
37          } catch (SQLException sqlex) {
38              os.writeObject(new Integer(-3));
39          } finally {
40              CJ.closeConnection(dbConnect,checkOutUpdate);
41          }
42      }
43      else {
44          os.writeObject(new Integer(-4));
45      }
46  }
47 }
```

UpdateServletJDBC

The example to perform an update to the database is very simple, partially because we are passing much of the work off to stored procedures in the database. We do need a constant, MSECDAY, to represent the number of milliseconds in a day. This value is used to determine the due date of a video checked out. Notice that there are no data members in this class. All of the variables are processed in one method to prevent any multithreading problems.

The only method in UpdateServletJDBC is doGet(). This method starts similarly to Query-ServletJDBC in that the parameters are read. In this case, we retrieve the customer ID into the variable customerStr and the title of the requested video in the variable movie. As in many of the previous examples, a ConnectionJDBC object is created by the servlet. This means we are not doing connection pooling as in QueryServletJDBC. If we assume the number of calls to this servlet is relatively small, then the overhead of creating the connections is not too bad. We are going to use a *CallableStatement* object, so we declare one in line 17. The *ObjectOutputStream* is created exactly as in QueryServletJDBC.

If the parameters are present, we use the ConnectionJDBC object to create a connection to an Oracle database in lines 22–24. Next, we create the *CallableStatement* object checkOutUpdate by using the *prepareCall()* method in lines 25 and 26. (Details about the *CallableStatement* interface can be found in Section 3.2.) The stored procedure used by this *CallableStatement* is place_order (see Section 6.3.3).

In order to use the stored procedure, we first assign values to the input parameters. There are three of them: the customer ID, the title of the movie, and the date the movie is due back. The first two placeholders are the parameters from the applet, while the third is created using the same process as in TransactionTableModel (see Section 5.3). We then register the out parameter as an integer in line 34. With all of the parameters set, we execute the update in line 35. After the update is complete, we retrieve the return value from the output parameter by using the *getInt()* method and send that value to the applet in line 36. If there is a problem, we return the value −3. If the parameters are not correct, we return the value −4. As always, we close the connection when we are finished, in line 40.

6.3.3   The Stored Procedures

The update requests have done very little so far, passing all of the work down to the database itself. Although that is great for the applet and servlet code, we now have to generate the code for the stored procedures. This example uses PL/SQL for Oracle, but we use as few DBMS-specific commands as possible. The command to create the stored procedures is in the file procedures.sql on the guide's web site.

PL/SQL Stored Procedure

```
1   create or replace procedure place_order (customer_in IN Orders.CustomerID%type,
2   title_in IN varchar2,
3   date_in IN Orders.DueDate%type,
4   value_out OUT Integer) as
5   temp integer;
6   tape_number Orders.TapeID%type;
7   new_order Orders.OrderNumber%type;
8
9   begin
10  select CustomerID into temp from Customers where CustomerID = customer_in;
11
12  find_title(title_in, temp);
13  if temp = -1 then
14  value_out := -2;
15  return;
16  end if;
17
18  available(temp, tape_number);
19  if tape_number = -1 then
20  value_out := -2;
21  return;
22  end if;
23
24  select max(OrderNumber)+1 into new_order from Orders;
25
26  insert into Orders values(new_order, customer_in, tape_number,date_in, '0');
27  commit;
28
```

```
29  value_out := 0;
30  exception
31  when no_data_found then
32  value_out := -1;
33  when others then
34  value_out :=-3;
35  end place_order;
36  /
37
38  create or replace procedure find_title(
39     title_name IN varchar2,
40     title_number OUT Titles.TitleID%type) is
41  begin
42  select TitleID into title_number from Titles where Title = title_name;
43  exception
44  when no_data_found then title_number := -1;
45  end find_title;
46  /
47
48  create or replace procedure available
49         (title_in IN integer,
50          tape_out OUT Tapes.TapeID%type) as
51  cursor available_cursor is
52  select TapeID from Tapes
53  where TitleID = title_in and TapeID not in
54  (Select TapeID from Orders where TitleID = title_in
55  and Status = '0');
56
57  begin
58  open available_cursor;
59  fetch available_cursor into tape_out;
60  if available_cursor%notfound then tape_out:=-1;
61  end if;
62  close available_cursor;
63  end available;
64  /
```

PL/SQL Stored Procedure

The stored procedure place_order has four parameters, just as the corresponding *CallableStatement* has four placeholders. The first parameter is called customer_in (line 1). It is an IN parameter and is the same type as the type for the CustomerID field in the Orders relation. The syntax for such a type is tablename.columnname%type. The second parameter is title_in, an IN parameter defined as a VARCHAR2, which is a string. The third parameter is due_date, and it is the same type as the Due_Date field in the Orders relation. It is also an

IN parameter. The fourth parameter, value_out, is an OUT parameter and is an integer. The keyword "as" separates the definition of the stored procedure from the body.

We also have three local variables, defined on lines 5-7. The variable temp is an integer we pass to other stored procedures. On the other hand, tape_number is of the same type as the tape ID field in the Orders relation. We will use this variable to insert the TapeID value into the database. Finally, new_order is of the same type as the OrderNumber field in the Orders relation. This variable will hold the primary key value for the new order.

To have a successful order, we must do four things:

1. Check that the customer is in the database
2. Find the title ID of the title
3. Find any available tapes of the title
4. Insert the new record into the Orders table

Line 10 performs the SQL query to determine if the customer_in parameter is actually in the Customers table. If it is, processing continues to the next line, but if it is not, an exception is raised. Although similar to Java exceptions, these database exceptions are totally independent and do not cause Java exceptions to be raised in a *CallableStatement*. The exception is processed on lines 30-32. Just as with Java, there are several types of exceptions. Line 30 marks the beginning of the part of the procedure for handling exceptions. The one we are interested in is "no_data_found." If no customer record contains the passed-in CustomerID, then the "no_data_found" exception is raised and the code following line 32 is executed.

If the CustomerID is valid, the next step is to determine if the movie title is valid. The place_order procedure calls another stored procedure, find_title (lines 38-46), to determine if the title is in the database. The procedure takes a string as an IN parameter and returns a variable with the same type as the TitleID. If the title is in the Titles relation, the corresponding TitleID is returned. Otherwise, the procedure returns −1. We test temp, the OUT parameter, to see if it is −1. If it is, we set value_out (the OUT parameter of place_order) to −2, and return (line 15). Line 16 ends the "if" clause, and if temp holds a valid TitleID, execution of the procedure continues with line 18.

The next step in our stored procedure is to find an available tape of the desired title. As expected, we use another stored procedure to find it. This time, we use the available procedure (lines 48-64), passing in the local variable temp, which holds the TitleID from the find_title procedure, and the local variable tape_number. The available procedure will set tape_number to either the TapeID of a valid tape, or −1, if no tape is available. Once again, we test the return value of the stored procedure in lines 19-22. As with the test of find_title, if available returns −1, we exit the stored procedure. Otherwise, we continue to the next step.

In order to insert a row into the Orders table, we must have an OrderNumber. Since OrderNumber is a primary key, we have to have a value that is not already in the table. A simple way to do this is to find the largest value and add 1 to it. Line 24 does exactly that. Although line 24 appears to be a straightforward select query, it has the clause "into new_order" in it. This clause causes the results returned by the query to be inserted into the variable new_order.

This clause can only be used if the query returns only one row. If more than one row is returned, we must use cursors.

We can now insert the new row into the Orders table. Line 26 is a straightforward SQL Insert statement, with local variables and parameters used to hold the values. Once the insert is successful, the stored procedure commits the transaction and sets the OUT parameter (value_out) to 0, indicating success.

Since the stored procedure resides at the database and not at the servlet, we might be tempted to forget about concurrent execution. However, databases have many transactions running on them at the same time. There are two possible problems with the stored procedure, even if the database enforces serializable executions.

The first problem is OrderNumber. If two transactions concurrently execute line 24, then both will receive the same value for new_order. Therefore, both will attempt to insert a row into the Orders table with the same primary key. The first transaction will succeed, while the next will raise an exception, "dup_val_on_index." In this multitiered example, this will cause the update to fail with a return code of −4. Ideally, this problem should be avoided by using an automatic technique for generating key values, such as a trigger or auto-increment function.

The second problem is even more insidious. If two requests for the same title are concurrently processed by the stored procedure, the available procedure will return the same TapeID for each request. Both requests would have the same TapeID inserted into the Orders table, and both clients would be told their order is complete. However, if only one copy of the tape remains, one customer will not be able to receive the video. To solve this problem, the entire Orders table can be locked at the start of the stored procedure. That way, only one instance of the stored procedure can be executed at a time. Clearly, this will degrade performance of the overall system. The other alternative is to have a business practice to compensate customers when this problem arises, similar to the practice of airlines when flights are overbooked.

The stored procedures available and find_title do not contain any concepts unique from those presented in the other examples, so I do not explain them here. Further information about stored procedures and *CallableStatements* is in Section 3.2.

6.4 **Going Beyond**

1. Modify QueryServletJDBC.java so that it dynamically creates *Connection* objects only when one is needed.

2. Modify QueryServletJDBC.java and ServletApplet.java so that the applet requests rows in blocks of N records, but displays them in blocks of M records, where M < N and both are parameters in the HTML file.

3. Modify QueryServletJDBC.java to include *ImageIcon* objects in the dataVector before the servlet sends the data to the applet.

4. The applet can be much more sophisticated in dealing with users. Extend ServletApplet.java so that whenever a customer requests a movie, it is placed in a "shopping cart." When the user clicks on the "Order" button, a *JTabbedPane* pops up with the users

cart. A "Purchase" button (active only when the shopping cart is visible) sends all of the requested movies to the servlet. Modify UpdateServletJDBC.java so that it can handle multiple requests and can send meaningful responses.

5. Modify ServletApplet.java so that a new customer can be added. When the customer ID box appears, allow the user to enter 0 if they don't have a number. A *JTabbedPane* then inputs all of the relevant data for the customer. Send the customer information to the server as a serialized object (you have to use the POST method instead of GET). Write a new servlet JDBC class to accept new customer objects in the doPost() method, and to return the new customer ID number.

6. Modify the entire multitiered system so that customers have passwords stored in the database. Require a customer to submit a password with an order. Process an order only if it has the correct password, and send an error message if the password is invalid. This will require modifying all three parts of the system.

chapter 7

How to Stay Current with JDBC

The ever-changing world of computer science waits for no one, and we must continue to learn more in order to be accomplished JDBC programmers. There are many concepts related to JDBC—applets, servlets, swing, and so on—that this guide is only able to cover lightly. For example, there are more SQL3 data types, other JDBC interfaces using the Java Naming and Directory Interface (JNDI) API and Java server pages (JSP), all of which are important for some applications. Security is an important topic whenever database capabilities are provided on the Internet, and this book only discusses the obvious problems. This chapter briefly covers these topics and provides references for further information.

7.1 JDBC 3.0

During the writing of this book, Sun released the JDBC 3.0 proposed final draft. JDBC 3.0 is scheduled to be part of the Java 2 Standard Edition, Version 1.4. According to the draft, JDBC 3.0 is "to round out the API by filling in smaller areas of missing functionality." As such, it does not have a major impact on an introductory guide such as this one, but further work will almost certainly require JDBC 3.0.

The current JDBC 3.0 API can be downloaded following a link on the guide's web page. The following is a collection of some of the changes that will impact the examples in this guide. This information is based on the summary of the changes between JDBC 3.0 and JDBC 2.0, as described in the April 2001 version of the draft.

- A single *Statement* object may have more than one *ResultSet* open at a time.

- Parameters will be passed to *CallableStatements* by name instead of placeholder position number.

- HOLD_CURSORS_OVER_COMMIT or CLOSE_CURSORS_AT_COMMIT can be added to the *Connection* methods to create *Statements*, *PreparedStatements*, and *CallableStatements*. The first value means a *ResultSet* object will not be closed after executing the *commit()* method, while the second value means the *ResultSet* object will be closed after executing the *commit()* method.

- *java.sql.Types.BOOLEAN* is added to the Types class.

- A new *ResultSet* method, *updateBlob()*, allows BLOBs to be updated.

- *ParameterMetaData* class allows JDBC to retrieve information about the parameters in a *PreparedStatement*.

- Added methods allow retrieval of auto-generated keys.

- *Savepoint* class allows JDBC to perform partial rollbacks.

Clearly, basic JDBC functionality will not be changed by the JDBC 3.0 API, but certain desirable features will be available.

7.2 javax.sql Package

The JDBC 2.0 API contains a group of classes and interfaces that are considered optional for JDBC 2.0 compliance, and they are included in JDBC 3.0 as well. These classes and interfaces are included in the javax.sql package. Some of the more interesting features are discussed here.

Much of the javax.sql package is based on using general *DataSource* objects instead of just databases. In fact, a *DataSource* object is similar to the *DriverManager* class in the java.sql package. The *DataSource* interface contains the *getConnection()* method for getting a *Connection* object, just like the *DriverManager* class. However, *DataSource* objects are designed to work with the JNDI. Thus, the *DataSource* objects are registered and accessed via the JNDI API. For further information about *DataSource* objects and the JNDI API, see [8].

The javax.sql package also has a mechanism for implementing connection pooling in a much more sophisticated manner than QueryServletJDBC.java. In connection pooling, when an application closes a connection, the resources are not released, but the connection is cached in memory. The next time a program requests a connection, a cached one is returned. This saves the work of opening and closing connections, thus reducing overhead. The javax.sql package implements connection pooling with *PooledConnection* objects. A *PooledConnection* object is implemented in the middle tier, such as the servlet in the example in Section 6.3.2. When a request is sent to the middle tier, if no connection is available, a new one is created. Otherwise, a *PooledConnection* object is created. This object then uses the *getConnection()* method to return a *Connection*.

Another interesting feature of the javax.sql package is the *RowSet* interface. *RowSets* are to the javax.sql package what *ResultSets* are to the java.sql package. In fact, the *RowSet* interface extends the *java.sql.ResultSet* interface. *RowSet* objects have several advantages over *ResultSet* objects. For example, *RowSet* objects do not require *Statements* in order to be connected to data. The *RowSet* interface contains the *execute()* method for pulling data into itself. The *RowSet* interface is also a bean, which is helpful to be part of a JSP environment. Finally, *RowSet* objects implement the *Serializable* interface, so they can be sent to applets or stored as files, while *ResultSet* objects cannot. The *RowSet* interface is one of the largest and most complex in the

JDBC API (exactly half of the classes and interfaces in the javax.sql package in JDBC 3.0 are related to *RowSet* objects); more information about them can be found in [8].

7.3 The Rest of java.sql

I cannot finish talking about the remaining parts of the JDBC API without mentioning that I did not even cover all of the components of the JDBC 2.0 API java.sql package. This section briefly covers the remaining interfaces and classes, along with a brief mention of when to use them.

As SQL has continued to expand, one of the improvements is its ability to represent more complex data. Specifically, there is an SQL type called ARRAY. The ARRAY type allows arrays to be stored as elements in a row. This could be useful with fields like address and phone number, where a single individual can have several of each. Arrays are accessed in much the same manner as BLOBs. There is a *ResultSet getArray()* method, which returns a *java.sql.Array* object. Within the *java.sql.Array* class, there is a *getArray()* method, which returns a Java array object. The *PreparedStatement* interface contains a *setArray()* method, which can be used to store arrays in an SQL array-type column.

Another expanded data type captured in java.sql is the *Clob* interface. CLOBs, character large objects, are useful for storing very large character constructs. Similar to the *Blob* interface, the *Clob* interface contains *getAsciiStream()* and *getCharacterStream()* methods to allow retrieval of the character data. CLOBs are useful for storing formatted data such as web pages or resumes in a database.

The interface *java.sql.Ref* is used as a reference within SQL to an instance of a structured type. The "oid" data type used in PostgreSQL to reference BLOBs is an example of a how a Reference type might be used. The *Ref* interface contains only one method, and that returns the type of the structured instance.

The interfaces *SQLData, SQLInput,* and *SQLOutput* are only used internally by the driver. Likewise, the class *DriverPropertyInfo* is only used to discover properties about the driver (not the database), so it is rarely used by programmers.

SQLWarning is a subclass of *SQLException*. Many database accesses cause potential problems but do not raise exceptions. These are reported as warnings. If desired, warnings can be retrieved by using the *getWarnings()* methods of *Connection, Statement*, and *ResultSet*. One specific warning is implemented as its own subclass of *SQLWarning*, and that is *DataTruncation*. *DataTruncation* is a warning when reading data, but it is an exception when writing data.

7.4 JSP

Java server pages (JSPs) are designed for dynamically generated Web content. A single JSP file contains both Java and HTML. When the file is requested, the web server executes the Java and outputs the created HTML. This means that the HTML file seen by the user does not physically exist on the server. Furthermore, JSP can use Java Beans to be as complex as needed. For example, we could write a bean to access a database and return particular values. Such a bean can be included with a JSP file.

JSP provides the security and performance similar to servlets in that the user does not see the Java code used to generate the data, and the user does not need to download the driver jar file. JSP also has an advantage over servlets in that true HTML tags can be used, which are much easier to create and maintain than a Java program. However, all of the actions performed with a JSP program must be done at the server side, and the user interface is limited to HTML (no *JTables* or other swing structures). The choice between applet-servlet structure and JSP depends on the complexity of the operation. The more complex the user interface, the more likely that applets are the right choice. An example of JSP is provided in the Appendix.

7.5 Security

One of the most crucial aspects of connecting a database to the Internet is security. Security applies both to information sent from the user to the database, and to the database itself. Information being sent to the database must rely on encryption to be secure. There are several layers of encryption possible. The correct choice for any application is specific to the application and is beyond the scope of this guide. However, some possibilities are

1. Secure Socket Layer (SSL): Using this connection encrypts the information sent to the web server (or servlet).

2. Post method: The parameters sent to the database appear in the URL if the Get method is used to retrieve the data. By sending parameters via the Post method, they are not as visible, and can be more effectively encrypted.

3. Objects: Finally, in our three-tier application, the applet can send objects to the servlet instead of simple character strings. These objects can be encrypted as well.

Security on the database end is based on not allowing attacks from undesirable parties. Recently, "denial of service" attacks have been a common means for hackers to shut down web sites. Connecting a database to the Internet provides an even better opportunity for these attacks, since every request must open a connection to the database. All databases limit the number of simultaneous connections, so once that limit is reached by undesirable requests, valid ones cannot get through. Preventing attacks like these and others is important for connecting databases to the Internet, but is beyond the scope of this guide. Further information can be found in [4].

Appendix

In this appendix, we present the other classes used by various programs in this guide. The classes are presented without commentary, although marginal documentation is provided. There are four files: The first is GUIJDBC, which provides the basic structure for the GUI used in many programs. The second is Communication, which is used to encapsulate the communication overhead between the applet and the servlet. The final two programs are part of a JSP example (see Section 7.4). The first is the HTML file with a form to send information to the servlet. The second is the JSP file used to generate the results. These two programs were provided by Guillermo Francia.

GUIJDBC

GUIJDBC

```
1   import java.sql.*;
2   import javax.swing.*;
3   import java.awt.event.*;
4   import java.awt.*;
5
6   public class GUIJDBC extends JFrame
7       implements ActionListener {
8       // Define the components and the layout
9       JLabel inputLabel = new JLabel("Customer ID Number");
10      JTextField inputText = new JTextField(" ",15);
11      JButton inputButton = new JButton("Query");
12      JPanel inputLayout = new JPanel(new FlowLayout(FlowLayout.CENTER,5,5));
13
14      public static void main(String args[]) {
15          GUIJDBC gJDBC = new GUIJDBC("Graphic JDBC Program");
```

```
16          gJDBC.show();
17          gJDBC.pack();
18      }
19
20      public GUIJDBC(String Title) {
21          super(Title);
22
23          // Add ourselves as a listener for the window closing
24          addWindowListener(new WindowAdapter() {
25                  public void windowClosing(WindowEvent we) {
26                      exitWindow(1); }
27              }  );
28
29          inputLabel.setLabelFor(inputText);
30          inputText.setHorizontalAlignment(JTextField.RIGHT);
31          inputText.addActionListener(this);
32          inputButton.addActionListener(this);
33
34          inputLayout.add(inputLabel);
35          inputLayout.add(inputText);
36          inputLayout.add(inputButton);
37
38          getContentPane().setLayout(new BorderLayout(5,5));
39          getContentPane().add("North",inputLayout);
40      }
41
42      // A default method, primarily used for testing.
43      public void actionPerformed(ActionEvent evt) {
44          String query = "Select Title, Type " +
45              "From Orders O, Titles T, Tapes V " +
46              "where V.TapeID=O.TapeID and T.TitleID=V.TitleID and " +
47              "Status = '0' and " +
48              "O.CustomerID= " + inputText.getText().trim();
49
50          ConnectionJDBC CJ = new ConnectionJDBC();
51          Connection dbConnect = null;
52          Statement dbStatement = null;
53          ResultSet dbRS = null;
54          try {
55              dbConnect = CJ.makeConnection();
56              dbStatement = dbConnect.createStatement();
57              dbRS = dbStatement.executeQuery(query);
58              presentResultSet(dbRS);
59          } catch (SQLException sqlex) {
60                  JOptionPane.showMessageDialog(null,sqlex.getMessage());
61          }
62          finally {
```

```
63              CJ.closeConnection(dbConnect,dbStatement);
64        }
65    }
66
67    // A default method, primarily used for testing
68    public void presentResultSet(ResultSet rs)
69        throws SQLException {
70        if (!rs.next()) System.out.println("No records for customer");
71        else {
72            do {
73                System.out.println(rs.getString("Title") + ": " +
74                                    rs.getString("Type"));
75                } while (rs.next());
76            }
77    }
78
79    // Exits the program upon closing the window
80    public void exitWindow(int i) {
81        System.exit(i);
82    }
83 }
```

GUIJDBC

Communication

Communication

```
1   import java.io.*;
2   import java.net.*;
3   import java.util.*;
4
5   public class Communication {
6       // url is the name of the servlet to connect
7       // paramCount is the number of parameters passed to the servlet
8       // ois is the stream for the return data
9       StringBuffer url;
10      int paramCount = 0;
11      ObjectInputStream ois = null;
12
13      public Communication(){}
14
15      public void setString(String URLString) {
16          url = new StringBuffer(URLString);
17      }
18
```

```
19      // Use URLEncoder class to handle conversion of blanks and other symbols
20      // First parameter follows '?', rest follow '&'
21      // All parameters are of the form "label=value"
22      public void addParam(String key, String value)
23          throws MalformedURLException {
24          if (url==null) { throw new MalformedURLException("No Servlet Defined"); }
25          String param = URLEncoder.encode(key) + "=" + URLEncoder.encode(value);
26          if (paramCount==0) url.append("?");
27          else url.append("&");
28          url.append(param);
29          paramCount++;
30      }
31
32      // Create URL based on values passed in
33      // Open URL connection to servlet
34      // Setup the input stream
35      public void connect()
36          throws IOException, MalformedURLException {
37          if (url==null) { throw new MalformedURLException("No Servlet Defined"); }
38          URL servlet = new URL(url.toString());
39          URLConnection con = servlet.openConnection();
40          InputStream is = con.getInputStream();
41          ois = new ObjectInputStream(is);
42      }
43
44      // Read something off the input stream
45      // If it is not an object (e.g., an integer) exception is thrown
46      public Object readObject()
47          throws IOException, ClassNotFoundException {
48          if (ois==null) { throw new IOException ("No Input Stream Defined"); }
49          return ois.readObject();
50      }
51
52      // Ends the connection and flushes the buffer in case multiple
53      // error messages in queue
54      public void disconnect()
55          throws IOException {
56          url = null;
57          paramCount = 0;
58          ois.close();
59          ois = null;
60      }
61  }
```

JSP Example

query.html

```
1   <html>
2   <head>
3     <title>eVid Online Video</title>
4   </head>
5   <body>
6   <center><h1>Search Movie Database</h1></center>
7   <hr>
8   <form action="GetTitle.jsp" METHOD="POST">
9   Keyword: <input type="text" name="keyvalue"><br>
10  <center>
11  <input type="submit" value="SEARCH">
12  <input type="reset" value="Clear">
13  <hr>
14  </form>
15  </body>
16  </html>
```

GetTitle.jsp

```
1   <!-GetTitle jsp file -->
2   <html>
3   <head><title>Movie Titles</title></head>
4   <%@ page language="java" import="java.sql.*" %>
5   <body>
6   <center><h1>Movie Titles Selection</h1></center>
7   <table align="center" border="1" width="400">
8   <tr>
9   <th>TITLE ID</th><th>TITLE</th>
10  <th>YEAR</th><th>PRICE</th>
11  </tr>
12  <%
13  String keyword=request.getParameter("keyvalue");
14
15  Class.forName("sun.jdbc.odbc.JdbcOdbcDriver");
16  Connection dbConnect = DriverManager.getConnection("jdbc:odbc:jdbc_book");
17  Statement dbStmt = dbConnect.createStatement();
18  ResultSet dbRS = dbStmt.executeQuery("Select TitleID, Title, Year, Price " +
19                  "from Titles where Title like '%" + keyword + "%'");
20  while (dbRS.next()) {
21          int id = dbRS.getInt("TitleID");
```

```
22            String title = dbRS.getString("Title");
23            int year = dbRS.getInt("Year");
24            double price = dbRS.getDouble("Price");
25   %>
26   <tr>
27   <td><%= id%></td><td><%= title%></td>
28   <td><%= year%></td><td><%= price%></td>
29   </tr>
30
31   <% } // end while
32   dbStmt.close();
33   dbConnect.close();
34   %>
35
36   </table>
37   <a href="query.html>Go back to main page</a>
38   </body>
39   </html>
```

GetTitle.jsp

References

[1] Cooper, J. *Comparing JSP, ASP and Servlets*. DevX: *www.devx.com/upload/free/features /javapro/2000/04apr00/jt0004/jt0004.asp*.

[2] Deitel, H., and Deitel P. *How to Program Java*. Prentice Hall, 1999.

[3] eMarketer.com: *www.emarketer.com/estats/20000808_activ.html*.

[4] Garfinkel, S., and Spafford, G. *Practical Unix and Internet Security*. O'Reilly, 1996.

[5] Hunter, J., and Crawford, W. *Java Servlet Programming*. O'Reilly, 1998.

[6] Nordhal, C. *Java Server Pages for the ASP Programmer*. ASP Today: *www.asptoday.com /articles/19991022.htm*.

[7] Sanders, R. *ODBC 3.5 Developer's Guide*. McGraw-Hill, 1998.

[8] White, S., et al. *JDBC API Tutorial and Reference,* second edition. Addison-Wesley, 1999.

Index

updateInt( ) method, 64
UpdateJDBC, 43-44
    actionPerformed( ) method, 44
    BatchUpdateJDBC vs., 47
    code, 43-44
    defined, 43
UpdateResultSetJDBC, 50-51
updateRow( ) method, 49
updates, 43-53
    batch, 45-47, 53

executing, 44
with *PreparedStatements,* 45
through *ResultSets,* 48-52
simple, 43-44
UpdateServletJDBC, 90-92
    CallableStatements, 90, 91
    code, 90-91
    defined, 84, 90
    doGet( ) method, 91
updateString( ) method, 49, 64

UpdateTableModel, 48-49
    code, 48-49
    defined, 49
    error message display, 49
    update( ) method, 49, 51
users, information presentation to, 15-31

Vector, 15, 16, 18, 19, 51, 71, 83
Vectors, 15, 16, 19, 28, 74, 83

CPSIA information can be obtained at www.ICGtesting.com
Printed in the USA
LVOW03s0245300814

401362LV00010B/221/P